Business Writing

Business Writing

BADEN EUNSON

BICENTENNIAL
1807
WILEY
2007
BICENTENNIAL

First published in 2007 by
John Wiley & Sons Australia, Ltd
42 McDougall Street, Milton Qld 4064

Office also in Melbourne

Typeset in Berkeley LT 11.3/14.3 pt

© Baden Eunson 2007

The moral rights of the author have been asserted

National Library of Australia Cataloguing-in-Publication data:

Eunson, Baden.

Business writing.

Includes index.
ISBN 9780731406494 (pbk.).

1. Business writing. 2. Business communication.
I. Title. (Series : Business tools series).

651.74

Cover image © Photodisc, Inc.

Author photo © David Sheehy

Wiley bicentennial logo: Richard J Pacifico

Printed in Australia by McPherson's Printing Group

10 9 8 7 6 5 4 3 2 1

Disclaimer
The material in this publication is of the nature of general comment only, and does not represent professional advice. It is not intended to provide specific guidance for particular circumstances and it should not be relied on as the basis for any decision to take action or not take action on any matter which it covers. Readers should obtain professional advice where appropriate, before making any such decision. To the maximum extent permitted by law, the author and publisher disclaim all responsibility and liability to any person, arising directly or indirectly from any person taking or not taking action based upon the information in this publication.

Contents

Preface

Why bother with communication? Sure, communication is a 'soft skill' that everyone talks about, but is communication that important when you need to be upgrading your skills and knowledge as you are developing your career? Well, actually, it is. All varieties of communication are among the best business tools you can have in your career toolkit.

A 2006 survey by Graduate Careers Australia, *Graduate Outlook 2006*, found that when employers were looking for graduates to hire, the technical competence of the graduates in their chosen field ran a poor second to the communication skills the employers were primarily looking for.

Much the same considerations apply even if you don't have a degree, or are already in your first or second career—time and again, those with good or great communication skills seem to have an advantage over those who don't.

Figure 1: 2006 survey by Graduate Careers Australia — factors favoured most by graduate employers

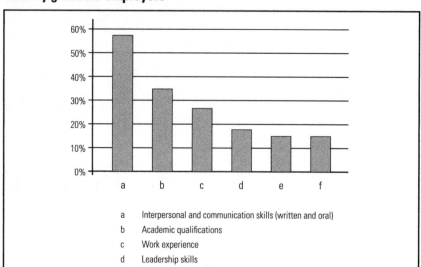

a   Interpersonal and communication skills (written and oral)
b   Academic qualifications
c   Work experience
d   Leadership skills
e   Passion/knowledge of industry/drive/commitment/attitude
f   Teamwork skills

Can such skills be learnt? Of course they can. The book you hold in your hands is part of the Business Tools series, a series that will help you use aspects of communication as tools to further your career, and possibly your own personal development.

Soft skills such as communication—in contrast to hard skills, such as number crunching and physical labour—are also known as generic, employability or transferable skills. This means that:

- while the technical knowledge you currently have may well be obsolete in five years' time, your soft skills will still be relevant in twenty or thirty years' time

- the transferable nature of soft skills will help you progress within your organisation and out of your current area of specialisation, and will help you move on to other organisations when the time is right for such a move.

Business Writing provides you with a range of techniques and approaches to writing paper and electronic documents, from memos, letters and reports, to emails and text for websites. I hope you find this book easy to read, and also hope that you can return to it as a tool and resource in your career as a communicator.

Baden Eunson
Melbourne
March 2007

Introduction

Business Writing looks at the different types of documents that are found in the workplaces of today and tomorrow. In the past decade, paper documents such as letters and memos have become less frequently used as email has emerged, but such documents are still important; in some situations in fact, they are more important than they ever were. Some trend predictors have told us that we are now in the age of the paperless office, but this is a myth—in most workplaces, there are now more paper documents about than there were previously.

Even when there is no need for hard-copy documents, the techniques of letter and memo writing that you will learn about in this book can be applied when writing any type of document—physical or electronic. In fact, some of the techniques of expression and persuasion can also be used in both conversation and presentations.

Good news letters (letters to customers and clients that say 'yes, we can help you') and bad news letters (letters to customers and clients that say 'no, we can't help you, but ...') are discussed as well. Various types of persuasive letters, exploring the processes of human motivation along the way, are also considered.

While letters are usually addressed to those outside the organisation, memos are generally addressed to people inside the organisation. Different types of memos for various situations are highlighted in this section, including situations when a hard or paper copy is directly preferable to an email.

I will look also at reports. Reports can be short or long, and can be used for a variety of communication situations. In particular, this chapter focuses on the longer form of the analytical or problem-solving report. Such a complex document presents numerous challenges, and many of your colleagues will do whatever they can to avoid writing reports. Such avoidance is hardly surprising—after all, these documents can be a big and time-consuming job. If you take up these challenges, however, and become known as someone who can write excellent reports, it will enhance your reputation considerably.

Finally, I will discuss a close relative of the analytical report—the tender, also known as the proposal or submission. A section on online writing closes *Business Writing*, covering both emails and website text.

Chapter 1

Letters 1—what they are and how to write them

One of the most important elements of business writing is writing letters. You may ask, 'Why should I bother with such an old-fashioned form of communication as letters?' There are many reasons why letters are still utilised; read on to find out why.

Letters—when, why and how

Letters are one of a number of genres we use as communicators. With the rise of email, it is commonplace to hear about 'the death of letter writing' in relation to both personal and professional communication. In spite of this, the letter is still very much alive—primarily because its advantages still outweigh its disadvantages, which are listed in table 1.1 (overleaf).

Table 1.1: advantages and disadvantages of letter writing as a channel of communication

Advantages	Disadvantages
Official status: many recipients will take a letter, especially on letterhead, more seriously than a fax or email	*Time cost*: it takes longer to plan, draft, write, edit and send a letter, via mail or courier, than to use email
Touch and keep: a letter can be handled, filed and stored without loss of quality	*Financial cost*: letters involve costs in labour, materials (printed letterhead is costly), postage/delivery costs, and creation and storage of copies
The personal touch: a signed or handwritten letter carries more weight and consequence for many recipients than a fax, email or telephone call	*Slow delivery*: letters sent via 'snail mail' involve longer delivery times than faxes or emails
Slow delivery: the weakness of relatively slow delivery can be a strength if the creation process leads us to take more care in the message's production—putting more thought into the words and ideas on the page	

> *You don't write because you want to say something, you write because you've got something to say.*
> F Scott Fitzgerald

New technology has increased our channels of personal and business communication, which now include physical and electronic methods such as letters, memos, reports, faxes, emails and SMS (short message service) via telephones. Technology changes, but certain principles of communication remain constant. We should never forget the 8Cs of written communication (see table 1.2).

> *The discipline you use to write things down clearly is the first step in making them real.*
> Lee Iacocca

Table 1.2: the 8Cs of written communication

As writers, we need to be ...	How?
1 Clear	The document should send a plain and unambiguous message
	It should not confuse or patronise the recipient
	It should aim to prevent or fix, not cause, communication breakdowns
2 Correct	The message should contain no factual errors
	All words, especially proper names, should be spelt correctly
3 Comprehensive	The message should include all critical information
	The recipient should not need to seek clarification because the writer has made assumptions about the recipient's knowledge
4 Concise	The message should be only as long as it needs to be
	The message should be only as complex as it needs to be
5 Credible	The message should be conveyed in a professional way
	Any opinions should be supported by facts
6 Considerate	The message should reflect the 'you' attitude (that is, a concern for the reader's needs and interests, rather than the writer's). The 'you' attitude is:
	Polite—demonstrating good manners and tact
	Practical—answering the recipient's question 'What's in it for me?' (that is, it gives the recipient an incentive to respond to, rather than ignore, the message) (see p. 50)
7 Courteous	The message should reflect respectful and civilised values
	It should not give the reader cause to take offence, or to take legal or retaliatory action
8 Conscientious	The message should meet the highest ethical standards
	It should contain no material unethically taken from other sources

Approaches to writing letters

Different approaches may be taken when writing letters, depending on their purpose. For example, it's useful to distinguish between direct and indirect approaches to the topic. Each pattern has its strengths and weaknesses.

The direct approach in a business letter is appropriate; for example, when we are able to give our readers what they want, while a more indirect approach may be taken when we are unable to do so or when conditions apply. We need to keep the direct/indirect distinction in mind when creating documents for different situations and recipients. Table 1.3 lists the direct and indirect patterns of letter organisation.

Table 1.3: direct and indirect patterns of letter organisation

Pattern	Approach	Strengths	Weaknesses
Direct	States primary message right away	Quick Honest Straightforward	Can seem abrupt Can alienate reader before writer has time to convey other messages
Indirect	Leads gradually towards primary message, which is couched within a sequence of minor messages	Can be a sensitive way of preparing reader for bad news Can be used to convey other messages before primary message	Can lead to waffle, evasion Can be seen as dishonest, manipulative

Before I turn to some of the techniques involved in composing letters, I will briefly look at matters of process — presentation, layout, formatting or information design, and conventions of wording and expression.

The elements of a letter

A letter contains various elements, some of them essential, others optional, depending on the circumstances. Within many organisations, these questions are determined by house-style conventions — 'the way we do things around here'. Communication conventions develop over time and vary considerably according to the organisational culture. People in organisations may often be unaware of the specific house-style conventions under which they operate until:

- someone decides it would be a good idea to write a house-style manual

- the organisation merges with another and is confronted with a different culture and with conventions that differ slightly or radically

- technological changes prompt writers to challenge current conventions.

Much of this section on document conventions is about details. Details can be boring, but when writers get one or several details wrong, the impact and effectiveness of the document is compromised. Attention to, or neglect of, detail sends out a message of its own, separate from but linked to the main content of the communication. Table 1.4 details the essential and optional parts of a letter.

Table 1.4: essential and optional parts of a letter

Essential	Optional
Sender's address	Subject line
Date	Attention line
Recipient's name and address	Security heading
Salutation	Reference details
Body of letter	Document initials
Close	Sender's contact details
Signature block	Enclosure details
	Copy details
	Headers/footers

Before laying out a letter form, you need to check your margins. On a standard A4 sheet (20 × 29.5 cm), it is conventional to set left and right margins at about 2 cm (horizontal dimension), and to allow about 4 cm at the top and bottom of the page. This will vary if letterhead is used. Letterhead—paper carrying a preprinted heading giving the organisation's name together with full address and contact details—is primarily a form of marketing and corporate image making. It is also relatively expensive to produce. For these reasons, most individuals don't use letterhead when writing personal letters.

On letterhead the sender's details (name, addresses and other organisational information) are usually printed at the top of the page and centred (sometimes centred at the bottom), with the date entered at the top left. In personal letters on non-letterhead, the sender's details are usually positioned at the top right, 3 cm to 4 cm from the top, with the date below.

Using the model letter in figure 1.1, I'm now going to analyse the various parts of letters.

Sender's address

The sender's address should include street name and number, or post office box or private bag number, suburb/city and postcode or other coding details required by postal authorities. If the letter is being sent interstate or overseas, state and national details should be included. If you are using letterhead, then the address and contact details are already given.

Date

Confusion sometimes arises about appropriate date styles because varying conventions apply in different parts of the world. As global communication increases, business communicators are increasingly encountering different forms and conventions. Therefore, the date style '06-07-08' can mean different things to different people. Different date styles are listed in table 1.5 (p. 9).

The International Standard ISO 8601 gives preference to the year-month-day (yyyy-mm-dd) system, but with the full year given, numbers less than ten starting with a zero, and separation made by dashes (for example, '2009-05-04' means the fourth day of May, 2009). This helps avoid day/month confusion and establish that 2009 and not 1909 is meant. The simplest way of avoiding such confusion, of course, is to write out the date in full (for instance, '4 May 2009').

Figure 1.1: elements of a professional, or letterhead, letter

CLEAN FOOD COMPANY Ltd

32 Ozone Way, Seaspray Park 8902

Telephone (06) 4921 3200   Facsimile (06) 4921 3201

www.cleanfood.com

Date

14 August 2008

Letterhead—contains sender's details

Recipient's name and address

Dr Martita Clemens,
    Chief Executive Officer,
    Acme Warehousing Systems,
    6 Enterprise Court,
    SEASPRAY PARK 8902

Subject line

Dear Dr Clemens:

Salutation

CLEAN FOOD AT ACME?

Congratulations on moving into the Seaspray Coast Industry Park.

Setting up a new operation means many worries and challenges, so food catering may not be your top priority at the moment.

However, when you have time to breathe, I urge you to think about getting your meals custom-catered through Clean Food Company. Ten other businesses in Seaspray do, and they are all happy with the service we provide. Five of these companies are big enough to have their own cafeterias, but choose to outsource their food and drink requirements through us.

Body of letter

So what do we provide? I attach a list and brochure of our wares, but in brief, we can supply you and your staff with cost-effective and nutritious food, twenty-four hours a day, seven days a week if needed.

Just imagine being able to choose from a variety of hot and cold foods at any time—and what foods! Our specialities include gourmet hamburgers, sushi, wholemeal pizza, cashew loaf, soy salads, fruit smoothies, exotic fruit salads, thirty-two varieties of cakes

Figure 1.1 _(cont'd)_: elements of a professional, or letterhead, letter

and biscuits, and fifteen types of coffee and tea. Over 50 per cent of our food and drink is organic in origin, and over 80 per cent is from non-genetically modified sources. We also go easy on the sugar, fat and salt.

We can provide biodegradable, use-only-once plates, cups and utensils, or full-grade crockery, glassware and utensils, which we clean for you. We can either cater into your premises, or your people can simply walk to one of our food wagons, which are stationed throughout Seaspray at various times of the day. You can order a custom menu for one or one hundred just by ringing us or logging on to our website. Most people spend less than ten dollars a day on a main meal plus dessert, and many use us for morning and afternoon breaks, as well as shift work meals. Need multiple courses of fine foods, with wines, silver service and waiting staff for entertaining your special clients? Not a problem.

Don't take my word for it, though. I'm biased! Talk to our satisfied clients and find out what they think. I attach a list of our contacts at businesses in Seaspray. I also enclose 20 × $10 value tokens which can be used at any of our wagons. Enjoy!

Please ring me if you have any queries about Clean Food Company's operation. I hope you find Seaspray is exactly what you need to make your business thrive.

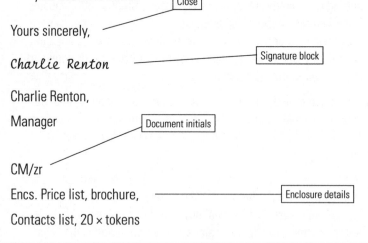

Close

Yours sincerely,

Charlie Renton

Signature block

Charlie Renton,

Manager

Document initials

CM/zr

Encs. Price list, brochure,

Enclosure details

Contacts list, 20 × tokens

Table 1.5: variations in dating systems

System	Countries using this style include	'06-07-08' means
Year-month-day	China, Japan, Korea, Hungary, Sweden	The eighth day of July, 2006
Month-day-year	United States	The seventh day of June, 2008
Day-month-year	United Kingdom, Australia, New Zealand, France	The sixth day of July, 2008

Recipient's name and address

The recipient's name and address are placed below the date, normally on the left-hand side of the page. In some cases a courtesy title or honorific will precede (Mr, Ms, Dr) or follow (MD, PhD, Esq., MP) the name. Role titles usually take capitals for major words. See table 1.6 for some examples of courtesy role titles.

Table 1.6: abbreviated courtesy titles/honorifics and role titles

Abbreviated courtesy titles or honorifics	Role titles
Mr, Ms, Mrs, Master, Dr, Professor, Monsignor, The Right Honourable, Reverend, Rabbi, Senator	Coordinator of Student Activities
	Manager, Operations
MD, PhD, Esq., MP	Team Facilitator
	Pastoral Care Advisor
	Minister for the Environment

Accuracy in relation to titles, names and addresses is vital. This is not only because accuracy will help a letter reach its destination, but also because people are very sensitive about their personal details—they do not appreciate it when correspondents are careless over these particulars. This is especially true for people with unusual names, so when in doubt, check. (Remember that, like dates, name sequences vary from culture to culture.) Think about how you feel when you receive a document that:

- has your courtesy title wrong
- has your gender wrong
- misspells your name
- confuses your first name with your last name
- has the wrong role title.

Don't hesitate to make a simple telephone enquiry to confirm these personal details. Any possible embarrassment or inconvenience this may cause you will be more than outweighed by the positive impact arising from the trouble you have taken to get it right will have on your reader. You have passed the first test: you have shown courtesy, consideration and care. You may well be the only correspondent this week, or month, to have done so.

Similarly, if a courtesy title is appropriate and your reader is female, find out whether she prefers to be addressed as Ms, Miss or Mrs. Alternatively, avoid such titles altogether. If unsure of the gender of the target reader, or the cultural conventions governing the name sequence, use the reader's full name (for example, 'Dear Lee Hoh').

Salutation

Whether or not the person you are writing to is the object of your affection, it is conventional to open letters with the salutation 'Dear [name]'. If your relationship is formal, or if this is the first time you have communicated, use the recipient's surname or family name. Once you have achieved some familiarity or rapport it is usual to use personal or given names. If unsure of the reader's gender, use the (only partly satisfactory) greeting 'Dear Sir/Madam' or 'Dear Madam/Sir'.

Body of the letter

The body of the letter contains the substance of the communication— your message. Its style and structure are largely determined by the kind of letter you are sending. Various types of letters are discussed in this and later chapters.

Close

Closes, or complimentary closes, are a way of terminating your letter with courtesy. Again, the wording you choose will vary according to the situation, and the tone appropriate to that situation. As with the salutation, you may feel slightly uncomfortable or even hypocritical in using the customary forms—especially with people who are not dear to you and for whom you have no sincere, faithful, respectful or true feelings. Unless you wish to dispense with such customs, however (as in the simplified letter format, p. 16), you should persevere. Think of the sometimes excessive chivalry of the traditional letter salutations and closes as marks of respect and civility in a world too often devoid of these qualities. Some closes you can use are shown in figure 1.2 (overleaf).

Signature block

The signature block contains the writer's signature. In business correspondence, it is usual to place this above the typed name (and title) of the writer. Sometimes a secretary or colleague may be empowered to sign on the writer's behalf. In these cases, this person signs:

1   the writer's name

2   the initials *p.p.* (Latin for *per procurationem*, meaning 'by proxy')

3   his or her own name.

Use this convention only when necessary. In some situations (for example, when the letter is personal or its impact profound), your reader may interpret this signature convention negatively ('He's so arrogant and insensitive he won't even take the time to write it himself').

Subject line

The subject line is a way of instantly telling the reader what the letter is about. It is placed between the salutation and the body, and is sometimes underlined or set in a different font. Email software packages have successfully borrowed this print document convention. Make sure the subject line accurately describes the message's content. Treat it as if you were writing a headline for a news story—grab your reader's attention without misrepresenting the message.

Figure 1.2: continuum of informal to formal closes

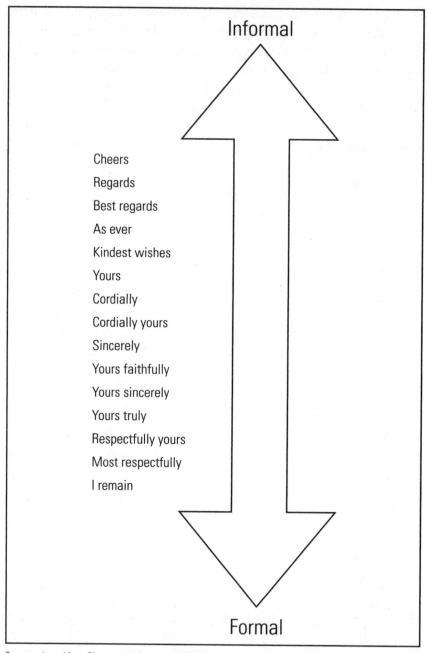

Informal

Cheers
Regards
Best regards
As ever
Kindest wishes
Yours
Cordially
Cordially yours
Sincerely
Yours faithfully
Yours sincerely
Yours truly
Respectfully yours
Most respectfully
I remain

Formal

Source: adapted from Chesterton, L (ed.) 1992, *Effective business communication*, Houghton Mifflin, Boston; Blake, G & Bly, R 1992, *The elements of business writing: a guide to writing clear, concise letters, memos, reports, proposals, and other business documents*, Longman, New York.

Attention line

In a large organisation it is not always clear who should handle a particular piece of correspondence. An attention line (for example, 'ATTENTION: JOE SMITH') is a way of increasing the probability of the letter reaching the right person. It is also useful if the role or position of the reader is the more significant factor (for instance, 'ATTENTION: STATIONERY PURCHASING MANAGER').

Security heading

Occasionally a writer wishes to ensure that only one person gets to read the letter. The probability of this can be maximised (although not guaranteed) by placing words such as 'PRIVATE AND CONFIDENTIAL' or 'FOR THE EYES OF JANE SMITH ONLY' on the letter and envelope.

Reference details

It is sometimes useful to mention a specific file number or other reference details, so that the reader can place the current communication in the context of earlier related documents. These details may take the form of abbreviations, codes or dates, and may relate to a reference system used by the reader, the writer or both parties. The reference line is normally placed above the body and after or opposite the salutation, sometimes in place of the subject line. It is common to underline this data or set it in a different font, or both:

Your Ref. As/ceZZ/2. Our ref. QWE/04

The subject, attention and reference lines are simple tools to facilitate the processing of information and are particularly convenient in ongoing correspondence.

Document initials

A common convention is to place the initials of the document's creator or creators at the bottom right-hand corner of each page. If one person dictates the document and another produces it, the initials of the principal are set in upper case, with the typist's initials following in lower case (for example, 'CFR/sw'). Today, even managers tend to do most of their own keyboarding. Increasingly, they are placing their own initials in the conventional lower left position, sometimes accompanied by a computer filename.

Sender's contact details

Senders will sometimes include their own contact details (for instance, telephone and fax extension numbers, email address or mobile phone number). Such details in letterhead-format documents can be placed just below the signature block. This is a personal touch, and readers often appreciate the fact that they can quickly contact the writer if necessary. Some writers (and organisations) are loath to do this, as it may make them 'too accessible'. Setting aside the fact that most recipients do not actually make direct contact (but feel comforted by the fact that they could if they wanted to), it should perhaps be asked just what is wrong with the culture of an organisation that feels that it is indeed possible to be 'too accessible'.

Enclosure details

If other documents are attached or enclosed in the envelope, it is conventional to alert the reader to this fact with an abbreviation ('Enc.' or 'Encs.') in the lower left-hand corner of the last page of the letter. Sometimes a brief description of the enclosed material is added.

Copy details

If copies of the current document are being distributed to others, it is customary to indicate this using the abbreviation *c.c.* (for 'carbon copy', a reference to the days when copies were made using carbon sheets in typewriters), followed by the names of those receiving copies (for example, '*c.c.*: John Shana, Lara Maxton').

Occasionally blind copies of a document are made. This means that copies are distributed without the knowledge of the person to whom the initial document is addressed. In this case, the initials *b.c.* or *b.c.c.* are added to the copies, although not to the original. Email packages also provide this feature.

Be careful when using blind copies. If the principal reader is alerted to their existence by the writer's inadvertence, it can make a very poor impression. It may often be safer simply to photocopy the document to send to your confidential audience.

Headers/footers

Occasionally writers will include a header or footer (an identifying line at the top or bottom of the page) on each page. These are particularly useful if the document is long. They may contain a coded summary of the content—the date, the writer's name and the page number. A typical header or footer looks like this:

Smythe insurance claim/4 May 2008/p. 2

A header or footer will not usually be included on the first page of printed letterhead.

Letter formats

The format used in letters is sometimes determined by an organisation's house style, which in turn reflects a consensus, or officially prescribed perception, of what looks good. The major formats are shown in table 1.7.

Table 1.7: common letter formats

Format	Features	Remarks
Full block	Each line begins at the left margin (that is, it is left justified). This includes date, address and signature details. This format can be typed rapidly, because the typist simply has to start from where the return or cursor is automatically placed after each line is completed	Some people dislike full block because (to their eyes) the document seems to lean to the left—it looks visually unbalanced
Modified block	The date, close and signature block are centred Full justification (words spaced to fill entire line) may be used to avoid perception of 'lopsided' left justification	Some believe this looks more balanced. Others prefer the simpler look of the full block. Centring is an automatic option with word processing software but can be a hassle with typewriters

Table 1.7 *(cont'd)*: common letter formats

Format	Features	Remarks
Traditional	Similar to full block or modified block, except that each paragraph is indented about 4–6 letter spaces	Vertical spacing between paragraph blocks often not used. More text can therefore fit on to a page, but it can look cramped
Simplified	Similar to full block, with all lines left justified. The salutation and close are dropped, however, with emphasis falling on the subject line	Clean and modern to some eyes, especially writers uncomfortable with traditional salutations and closes. To other eyes, however, it can seem impersonal. Often uses open punctuation

Source: adapted from Lahiff, J & Penrose, J 1997, *Business communication: strategies and skills*, 5th edn, Prentice-Hall, New Jersey.

Paragraphing

Some writers prefer to mark the beginning of a new paragraph by indenting from the left margin, while others prefer to leave the new paragraph flush with the left margin, but separated from the previous paragraph by a line space. Some choose to combine these approaches, although this duplication tends to annoy some readers.

Punctuation

A letter writer using a traditional punctuation style will include commas after each line of name and address details, full stops or periods after abbreviations, and a comma or colon after the salutation. The open punctuation style dispenses with these punctuation marks, while maintaining normal punctuation in the body (see table 1.8). Some writers choose to mix traditional and open punctuation styles.

Letter look—corporate identity and marketing tool

Many organisations take the look of their correspondence, both external and internal, very seriously. They believe—not without justification—that the appearance of their correspondence sends powerful messages about the professionalism of the organisation.

House-style guides for employees are designed to introduce a consistent standard to all correspondence.

Table 1.8: traditional versus open punctuation

Traditional punctuation	Open punctuation
Dr. J. A. Smith,	Dr J A Smith
44, Carrolls Way,	44 Carrolls Way
Middletown, 7451	Middletown 7451
Dear Dr. Smith:	Dear Dr Smith

Try it yourself

1   Collect a range of letters including business correspondence and junk mail. Analyse them in terms of the various elements we have considered. How effective are they? If you were to reformat them, what changes would you make?

2   If you ran your own business, or held a position within an organisation, how would you choose to lay out your letters? What formatting, paragraphing and punctuation would you use? Why?

Chapter 2

Letters 2—giving good news and bad news

Chapter 1 looked at various letter formats. This chapter explores some different categories of business letters, such as routine messages (and why you should not adopt a 'just routine' approach to them), good news letters (where the message you are sending is one your reader wants to read) and bad news letters (where the message you are sending is one your reader doesn't necessarily want to read).

Letters—the message

Chapter 1 focused on how letters can be laid out, what conventions should be followed, why they are still a valid form or genre of writing in this age of email, and why letters are perhaps more important than ever in certain circumstances. Chapter 2 explores some of the different categories of business letters.

Routine messages

Organisations have developed a number of ways of conveying routine messages to customers or clients. These include form letters, postcards, acknowledgement slips, and the 'with compliments' slip or business card that accompanies pamphlets, brochures or other promotional literature. Form, or 'canned', letters are standard letters fitting into a template that are personalised via word processing software. Sometimes this process is undetectable; at other times, particularly in much junk or spam mail, it is all too noticeable.

Many people don't ordinarily appreciate receiving junk or canned letters, so such communications often do more damage than good to the organisation that sends them. Why do organisations persist in using such means? Simple: it's cheaper (or it appears to be cheaper). It costs the organisation time and money to personalise letters to prospective customers or clients, or even to modify a form letter.

The non-routine—giving the news

Non-routine letters are often sent in situations in which routine replies are not expected. Again, these documents cost time and money, but if they are well designed, this investment will pay off. This is because, in a real sense, *every letter is a sales letter*. That is, every document that an organisation sends out is a marketing tool for that organisation, conveying more than the mere facts of the communication. For example, it sends a message about whether the organisation is courteous or rude, competent or derelict, up-to-date or obsolete. So there is no such thing as 'just a letter'—letters can make or break the good name of an organisation or individual.

Good news letters—when they want to read what you write

Good news letters convey positive messages to readers ('we can help you'), while bad news letters convey negative messages. *Bad news letters* are often more challenging to write, but that does not mean good news letters cannot be written badly. (See also pp. 84–85.)

Good news—using the direct approach

The ideal structure of the good news letter is as follows:

- Give the good news right away.

- Background the good news; if appropriate, use the letter to promote other products or services of the organisation.

- Close in an upbeat way.

Applying an indirect structure by burying the good news within other material risks irritating the reader. This irritation is compounded if the writing style is obscure or waffly. Overlong business letters of this type are usually ineffective.

Be wary, however, of committing the opposite sin—that of being direct to the point of abruptness, failing to place the message in context, and therefore communicating ineffectively because too few words are used. This is not so much 'plain English' as 'pain English'. Examples of effective and ineffective openings are shown in table 2.1.

Table 2.1: ineffective and effective openings

Ineffective opening: too wordy	Effective opening	Ineffective opening: too brief
'Dear ...	'Dear ...	'Dear ...
Thank you for your valued letter of the 19th. It is always a pleasure to hear from our customers, and your letter was no exception. Since the foundation of this institution in August 1895, customer service has been our watchword.	Thank you for your letter of 19 June, in which you enquire whether Protector offers alternatives to single annual premiums.	Yes, we do offer monthly payment of premiums. Details are in the attached brochure.'
I refer to your letter, in which you ask whether we at Protector Insurance allow incremental or fractional payments of premiums. We calculate our premiums according to various formulae ...'	Yes, we do offer a range of payment options. These are ...'	

Many attempts to communicate are nullified by saying too much.
Robert Greenleaf

Opening words thanking the reader for his or her letter, phone call, fax, email or other communication are not simply ritual courtesies (although in the modern world such courtesy has much to recommend it); they also remind the reader of the nature of the original enquiry. This is not to suggest readers are idiots who need to be reminded of everything they have written or said. The point is that they may have made five, ten or fifty enquiries within a week, on numerous matters, to many organisations and individuals. It is inappropriate and potentially confusing, then, to respond as though engaged in a real-time conversation.

Indeed, there is no guarantee that the letter will be opened by the person who made the first contact. In some organisations, it is standard practice for one individual—someone in the mail office or central registry, a secretary, a personal or administrative assistant—to open mail addressed to another person.

The introductory comments, therefore, should briefly orientate the reader to the issue at hand, before setting out the substantive message. The writer who neglects this introduction may be perceived as discourteous, impatient, rude or simply disorganised.

An effective way of reconciling the need to orientate the reader with the need to convey the good news as soon as possible is to use a subject line as shown in figure 2.1.

Figure 2.1: example of a subject line

Dear …

Your letter 19 June: Protector premium rates

Yes, we do offer monthly payment of premiums …

Bringing good news—what not to do

Good news should be conveyed with speed, empathy and good grace. Such messages can be compromised by:

- lateness

- communication of the writer's boredom or lack of empathy

- communication of resentment or a grudging attitude.

Good and bad examples of a good news letter are provided in figures 2.2 (p. 24) and 2.3 (pp. 25–26).

Communicating bad news—when they don't want to read what you have written

One of the shortest words in the English language, no, is a word many of us have difficulty saying. It may suggest negativity, inadequacy, unhappiness, anger or conflict, and few of us are happy with such situations or emotions. In writing workplace documents, we sometimes have to break bad news to our readers, which means saying no. Such situations might involve any of the following scenarios:

- A customer has asked for credit or for an increase in credit.

- An applicant has applied for a job.

- A client has requested an adjustment, such as a refund or product return.

- Someone has ordered a product or service that is no longer available.

- A telemarketer has requested a donation to a cause.

- A friend has asked us to attend or speak at a social gathering.

- An employee seeks approval for an idea or project.

- Someone has submitted work (a working model, a pilot study, a manuscript) in the hope that we will develop, produce or publish such work.

Letting them down gently—the indirect approach

Conveying a bad news message often requires the formality of a mailed letter. Sometimes the news is sent by fax or email, but this channel choice does not excuse a rushed, garbled or inconsiderate communication.

Figure 2.2: an ineffective good news letter

CLONE POWER

Suite 39 Rintrah Industrial Park Claymore 23121 Freedonia
Telephone (615) 1233 4352 Facsimile (615) 1233 4354
www.clonepower.com Customer service info@clonepower.com

March 14, 2008

Ms Monica Zalecki,
Supervisor,
Administration Services,
Cogito University,
Smithfield 20114

Dear Ms Zalecki:

We often get complaints from customers, although very few of them, we find, have any foundation.

We subjected your *Quill* packages to intensive scrutiny, with two software engineers working on it for four hours to determine whether the packages were in the same condition as they were when they left our premises. We installed the packages onto four machines we keep especially for this purpose (each machine has a particular combination of hardware and operating system faults). Two of the machines replicated the faults you described in your letter (files lock up after 33 000 bytes, endnotes are unstable), while two did not. We then installed the packages on two new, optimally functioning machines, and found that the faults appeared intermittently.

Your cheque for $1296 is enclosed. Please ensure that it is banked within five working days.

Yours sincerely,

Malcolm Bickstaff,
Service Manager

Enc.

Annotations:
- Suspicious, hostile attitude — inference that customer is wrong
- Self-centred approach: 'We' attitude, not 'you' attitude
- No preamble, identifying what the situation is
- Detail that is irrelevant to customer
- Finally, the good news — expressed abruptly, ungraciously

Figure 2.3: an effective good news letter

 CLONE POWER

Suite 39 Rintrah Industrial Park Claymore 23121 Freedonia
Telephone (615) 1233 4352 Facsimile (615) 1233 4354
www.clonepower.com Customer service info@clonepower.com

March 14, 2008

Ms Monica Zalecki,
Supervisor,
Administration Services,
Cogito University,
Smithfield 20114

> A straight refund may satisfy customer, but may leave customer discontented with product. Option of replacement and upgrades gives choice, and builds goodwill.

Dear Ms Zalecki:

Thank you for your letter of 3 February, enclosed with the four copies of our *Quill* multi-user word processing package.

I am pleased to offer you two options:

> Direct approach: good news given right away

1   A refund cheque for $1296

2   Replacement copies of your *Quill* packages, all four having been bench-tested by our software engineers, together with 12 months' free online help on our *Quill* toll-free number.

The replacement copies or the cheque will be sent to you, by courier, at no charge to you. Just ring me direct on 1500 419 2331 and tell me how I can best help you.

> No mention of guilt, who is to blame—problem is solved, not dwelt upon

The faults you discovered were most extraordinary, and will help us to refine Version 3.3, scheduled for release in June. (Should you choose to accept replacement copies of the Version 3.2 packages, we will give you free upgrades.)

I apologise for the delays in your workload that have been caused by this glitch.

> 'You' attitude—minimal detail of writer's concerns

In your letter you mentioned that one of the faults encountered in the *Quill* packages was the instability of templates for forms—an important factor, as you need to design many forms. The *Quill* package is good for

Figure 2.3 *(cont'd)*: an effective good news letter

designing forms, but specialists such as yourselves may need a more high-powered package, such as *QuillFormz*. This package gives you over 200 templates, ninety-two more fonts and electronic form-filling capacity linking to databases. I attach a brochure for your interest.

Thank you for your interest in Clone Power products.

Yours sincerely,

Malcolm Bickstaff

Malcolm Bickstaff,
Service Manager

Enc.

> Flattery, attempt at further sales promotion

The communication principles for letters we will examine here are equally valid for messages transmitted electronically, and indeed for bad news conveyed verbally.

To convey bad news effectively, whether delivering the message in writing, over the phone or in person, it is useful to write out a script to help you navigate a potentially unpleasant situation.

Most bad news messages are best conveyed using the indirect approach, which means the bad news is initially withheld. Why should we use such an approach? In the interests of clear, honest and time-effective communication, why not just tell it like it is, in a few brief, polite words, and get on with other things? Such honesty has much to recommend it, but the bringer of bad news has to be careful. In workplace documents, we break bad news to people in an indirect way for a number of reasons:

- *Common courtesy and empathy*. Sensitive communicators put themselves in the place of the recipient, asking the question: how would I feel if I received this?

- *Tact and taking it personally*. One of the most futile pieces of advice we can ever give anyone is 'don't take this personally'. We tend to take most things personally, and this is particularly the case with bad news. Many of us will take a denial of credit or news that we didn't get the job we applied for as a sign of personal failure or rejection. In other words, bad news messages can easily provoke powerful emotional reactions. Such situations call for considerable tact, keep in mind the old saying—'making a point without making an enemy'.

- *Maybe there is some good news*. Bad news is not always a catastrophe. Just because we cannot give the reader what he or she wants to hear at this time does not mean we cannot offer something, either now or in the future. If, however, we place this offer after a brutally direct bad news opening, the reader may be so upset as to be in no state of mind to grasp the consolation. Hot blood and understanding tend to be inversely related.

With bad news messages, then, we use the indirect approach because it is courteous and sensitive. Also, it is a practical way to ensure that our total message gets through, undistorted by premature negative emotional reactions.

If you want their business, don't give them the business

We also need to consider the longer term effects of such emotional reactions. As already noted, in a very real sense, all documents are sales documents. We send letters and emails to customers or others outside our workplace, and we send memos and emails to people inside our workplace: let's therefore think of our colleagues as internal customers. When we write to our customers, both internal and external, we are in fact sending not one but two messages:

- *The explicit or surface message*: 'Here is my presentation of facts and opinions about the situation/problem we are both familiar with'.

- *An implicit or hidden message*: 'I am a competent person: I solve problems well'. (Or, 'I am an incompetent person: I solve problems badly'.) Also, 'I am a sensitive person: I am sympathetic to your needs'. (Or, 'I am an insensitive person: I am unsympathetic to your needs'.)

If we are unaware of the implicit, hidden messages we send, then our current communication with this customer may be our last. This is what is meant by the idea that all documents are sales documents. We may not think we are selling something when we write documents that are not specifically sales oriented, but in fact we are—implicitly we are selling ourselves, and the organisation we represent. And if you have to sell yourself, don't sell yourself short.

In this selling process, if we do not create and preserve customer goodwill, then we must surely create ill will. Many of the customer's impressions of an organisation—both good and bad—come not from face-to-face or telephone transactions, but through correspondence, and a good deal of that correspondence consists of bad news letters.

A rule of thumb is to presume that any business communications you write may be handed around, photocopied, pinned up on a noticeboard, faxed—in short, they may reach an audience much wider than the person to whom they were sent. You should aim to be the initiator of a chain of good impressions rather than that of a succession of bad impressions.

Being the bearer of bad news—how to do it well

Certain patterns of expression can be used in responding to a range of bad news situations. These patterns offer ways of conveying the bad news indirectly, with tact and sensitivity. Be wary, however, of adopting an unthinking, formulaic approach—many readers will detect such insincerity, and will find it as offensive as a blunt, rude one-line note.

Kisses, kicks, buffers and sandwiches

As has been noted, it is good elementary psychology to embed a bad news message inside a more positive communication. This means opening, and probably closing, your letter with good news or neutral information. This approach is sometimes called the bad news sandwich approach, in which the bad news is surrounded or buffered by other material, or the blow or kick you deliver is softened by the kisses that precede and follow it (see table 2.2).

Table 2.2: the bad news sandwich

Section of sandwich	Effect
Buffer	Kiss
Bad news	**Kick**
Buffer	Kiss

A buffer of more positive words and ideas will help soften the blow of bad news. Opening buffers are used to:

- express appreciation
- restate the situation
- explore common areas of agreement
- offer reasons or explanations
- offer alternatives.

Buffers can be used separately and sequentially, or can be combined in a variety of ways, depending on your style preferences.

Appreciation buffers

Appreciation is usually expressed in the opening remarks as shown in table 2.3.

Table 2.3: expressions of appreciation

What is appreciated	How expressed
Efforts of recipient in having written/made contact	'Thank you for taking the time to notify us of the difficulties you have been experiencing with your...'
Good taste of recipient in having chosen our product	'We appreciate your interest in the Excelsior range of marine insurance policies...'

Restatement buffers

Restating the situation allows you, the writer, not only to put off the bad news but also to define the parameters of the issue, or just what it is that you and the reader are concerned with. Perceptions of a situation can vary from individual to individual, and your reader may see things differently from you, so it is worth going through this exercise. The details of a situation may, of course, already be summarised succinctly in the subject line, but a restatement in the text of the letter will further clarify the matter. Restatements are often combined with appreciations, for instance, 'Thank you for contacting us regarding your order of 6 June for 32 gross of our Kaylite S30 metabolic transducers ...'

Agreement buffers

It is useful for the writer to express some type of agreement in the opening of a bad news letter, even though all bad news letters are ultimately about disagreement (that is, the writer disagrees with the recipient about what should finally be done in a particular situation).

Disagreement is about people having differing views or areas of interest, and it often involves a measure of unpleasantness. Finding an area of agreement means finding some common interest between writer and reader; if this can be achieved, then the unpleasantness can be neutralised. Typical agreement statements are:

- 'We agree that account fees can initially be quite irritating to our customers, as savings account banking has always been a "free" service in this country ...'

- 'You are right to expect that our drill bits, when operated within normal tolerances, will deliver the performance people have come to expect from the market leader product ...'

Such statements aim to establish a rapport with readers, demonstrating that the writer is on the same side as the reader. This can create a foundation of trust that can perhaps be used to explore alternative solutions to the reader's problem.

Notice that these statements offer partial or conditional rather than total agreement. Almost certainly the bank customer does not think of bank fees as 'initially ... quite irritating' but rather as permanently infuriating and something that should be abolished forever. Similarly, the astute drill user (or abuser) will have detected the hedging or qualification in the words 'when operated within normal tolerances', which may well form the basis of the 'no' message to come. The writers of such statements have probably taken the initial customer comments or complaint and have edited them or modified them to convey a specific sentiment.

When using appreciation and agreement buffers, it is important that writers:

- convey cordiality, but do not give the false impression that good news is to come (unless it is)

- do not come across as sycophantic or crawling, dishonest or sarcastic

- do not twist the readers' own words in such a way that readers feel manipulated or suspect that the writers are being hypocritical and devious (lying through their smiles).

Explanation buffers

It is best to give your reasons for saying no before actually saying it. Not only can this help to soften the blow, but it helps to create a context in which the refusal will seem more reasonable. When giving explanations or reasons, consider the following guidelines:

- *Don't over-rely on official or company policy.* This position translates as 'we won't because we don't'. There may be good reasons for the policy, but applying it arbitrarily and unconditionally comes across as impersonal and bureaucratic. Each person believes that he or she is an exception to the rule, rather than an obedient, unthinking cog in a vast machine. Always put yourself in the shoes of the recipient—how would you feel if you read this?

- *Try to demonstrate some benefit of the policy.* It's a cliché to say that 'rules benefit us all', but sometimes this can be clearly demonstrated in a non-dogmatic way. If this can be done (and it won't always work), then do it. Some sample rules and applications are shown in table 2.4 (overleaf).

- *Don't talk down to the reader.* A patronising tone, like the 'company policy only' approach, demeans the reader. Assertions such as 'our vast experience over twenty-six years has shown us that this is the correct course' and 'we know what's best for our customers' may be true, but these statements should be demonstrated rather than declared.

Table 2.4: rules and applications

Rule	Unacceptable action sought by customer	Benefit for customer by observing rule
Every car should be brought in for a service inspection regularly (every six months); if this is not done, then the insurance contract ceases to provide coverage	Payment for repairs, even though the car has not been brought in for regular inspection	Regular inspections help to identify problems early, meaning minor faults do not develop into major ones requiring expensive repairs
Any clothing returned must be in perfect condition	Return of suit with food stains on it	The store can be trusted to sell only garments that have not been worn or damaged by others

- *Don't apologise.* Or at least keep apologies to a minimum. An apology may form part of the rituals of courtesy, but it can also sound defensive, suggesting the writer is not completely sure of his or her ground, and that the situation may therefore still be open to negotiation (the no that might mean yes). An apology emphasises the negative rather than the positive aspect of the communication; it can also widen the gulf between writer and reader—sympathy is a poor substitute for problem solving. Don't apologise—explain.

- *Don't make the explanation overlong.* The reader may feel that you are beating about the bush or waffling rather than getting to the point. This may well be a correct perception. Cut a long story short and use the explanation as a transition to the bad news.

- *Loose lips sink ships.* Be careful not to reveal commercially sensitive details, or information that could demonstrate culpability or inconsistency on the part of your organisation.

The meat of the sandwich—telling the bad news

The inevitable cannot be delayed any longer. There comes a time when you really have to tell the bad news, and this is it. If the explanation buffer has been well developed, then the shock will not be so great. When saying no, consider the following guidelines:

- *Avoid predictable negative transitional words.* These signal words (for instance 'however', 'but', 'nevertheless') almost always provoke a powerful negative response from readers, and can often undo all the good work that you have done in developing the explanation buffer.

- *Put a sandwich in a sandwich.* Place the 'no' sentence in the middle of a paragraph—as a sandwich within a sandwich, if you like. Place this paragraph in the middle part of the middle section of the letter.

- *Use the complex sentence technique.* Complex sentences are comprised of one main or independent clause, and one or more subordinate or dependent clause. The bad news is linked with other material—reasons, perhaps, or more positive alternative outcomes. People usually pay most attention to the main clause in a sentence. Messages tend to have a diminished impact if they are buried in subordinate clauses. Therefore it makes sense to put the bad news in the subordinate clause, and give greater emphasis to the more positive main clause (figure 2.4).

Figure 2.4: the complex sentence technique in bad news letters

Less effective complex sentence: bad news in main clause; other material in subordinate clause	More effective complex sentence: other material in main clause; bad news in subordinate clause
We cannot extend credit facilities to you at this time, although we will be able to review this decision if you can obtain long-term employment	While we cannot extend credit facilities to you at this time, we will be able to review this decision if you can obtain long-term employment
Your order cannot be processed at this time, although we may be able to supply you with a generator on a temporary basis	Although your order cannot be processed at this time, we may be able to supply you with a generator on a temporary basis

Source: adapted from Wells, W 1988, *Communications in business*, 5th edn, PWS-Kent, Boston.

- *Avoid 'hot button' words.* All words have various connotations or meanings. Words that sound harmless enough to you may in certain circumstances cause offence to others. Try to be sensitive to such possibilities. Of course, some words are unequivocally disrespectful or 'hard' and should be avoided. Not only is it bad manners to use such words, but it may also give cause for legal action to be taken against you. At the least, strong language will have negative public relations payoffs for your organisation. Always try to use respectful, 'soft' alternatives (see table 2.5).

Table 2.5: soft words and hard words — becoming sensitive to connotations

Hard word	Soft word
Crisis	Problem, situation
Refuse	Decline
Abandon	Relinquish
Cancel, quit	Forgo
Prevent	Preclude
Delayed	Are not yet available
	Will now not be available until ...
Bad risk	Do not satisfy all of our current criteria
Not good enough, inferior	Do not match our immediate requirements
Abused, wrecked	When tested, showed an extraordinarily high degree of wear and tear
Desperate	Concerned
Terrible, pathetic, outrageous, disgusting	Unacceptable

- *Avoid euphemisms.* At the other extreme from 'hot button' words are euphemisms. Euphemisms are used to describe unpleasant things in the most pleasant, diplomatic way possible. Thus a euphemism for 'dead' is 'passed away', while a euphemism for 'unemployed' is 'between contracts'. Euphemisms can sometimes be tactful, but they can all too easily be perceived as hypocritical gobbledegook. Wherever possible, choose plain English alternatives to euphemistic constructions (see table 2.6).

Table 2.6: euphemisms and plain English alternatives

Euphemism	Plain English alternative
'It is not possible at this juncture to facilitate reimbursement ...'	'We cannot give you a refund ...'
'It is not possible for the current employer–employee relationship to be sustained in the immediate future ...'	'Your employment with us is terminated ...' 'You are dismissed from your position ...'
'Inflation-driven retail charge adjustment'	'Price increase'
'Appears to have experienced a retrogradation in optimal performance parameters'	'Has been damaged'

- *Refer to groups or situations rather than to individuals.* Referring to the reader using second-person pronouns ('you', 'your') can sometimes convey an accusatory tone. It also emphasises the isolation of the reader from the writer, or even from the community in general. Whenever possible, include rather than exclude. Readers will often feel less threatened if you refer to them as part of a wider group ('you and other retailers', 'in fairness to all our retailers', 'in everyone's best interests') or as participants in wider situations ('in the current economic circumstances').

- *Use the passive voice.* When a person uses the evasive passive voice, we have every reason to believe they are seeking to avoid responsibility. The active voice is more direct and personal, and therefore preferable. Sometimes, however, the active voice may seem confrontational, and a passive construction, particularly an impersonal or agentless one, will help to soften the blow of the bad news (see table 2.7 on p. 36).

Table 2.7: active versus passive constructions

Active voice	Passive voice
'I found that…'	'It was discovered that…'
'You have not maintained the equipment correctly…'	'The equipment has not been maintained correctly…'
'We cannot refund the amount…'	'A refund cannot be made…'

- *Use subjunctive mood.* Mood is a property of verbs. Unlike the indicative and imperative moods, the subjunctive mood conveys types of conditionality, such as wishes, recommendations, indirect requests and speculations. The subjunctive mood is less confrontational than other moods and, like the passive voice, can help to make expression more indirect (see table 2.8).

Table 2.8: use of mood

Imperative/indicative mood	Subjunctive mood
'Pay by the 10th June…'	'We would be able to process this if you could pay by 10 June…'
'I cannot reverse this decision…'	'I wish that I were able to reverse this decision…'

Kisses and buffers again—creating silver linings

We have already noted the benefits of offsetting bad news with more positive information. Bad news relates to what you *cannot* do for the reader; good news relates to what you *can* do. Is there anything positive you can extract from an unpleasant situation? What silver linings can be found in the clouds hanging over your reader?

- If you cannot give a person credit facilities, can you give details of alternatives, such as lay-by/lay-away plans or discounts for cash purchases?

- If you cannot give a refund on an item, can you offer a trade-in allowance on another item or a discount on a further purchase?

- If you have to dismiss someone, can you offer them retraining or at least facilities (desk, phone) so they can hunt for another job?

It is not always possible to create options or alternatives, but whenever it is, be creative. Sometimes the alternative may prove to benefit the customer even more than the original outcome sought—one door closes, another opens.

Writing technique and the bigger picture—silver linings and top brass

Here we leave letter-writing technique for the moment to enter the realm of organisational policy. It is vital that management recognise the importance of offering options to both customers and staff. Silver linings can only be created by top brass. Offering options is a crucial policy area for several reasons:

- it is an ethical and compassionate strategy

- it helps to avert negative public relations outcomes for the organisation

- it gives the organisation a strategic marketing edge over its competitors who fail to recognise the wisdom of such an approach.

Table 2.9 provides an overview of techniques for conveying bad news.

Table 2.9: techniques for conveying bad news

Letter	Use buffers, sandwich, kiss–kick–kiss approach (appreciation, restatement, agreement, explanations).
Paragraph	Embed bad news in central paragraph (sandwich approach).
Sentence	Use complex sentence technique—bad news in subordinate clause, alternative in main clause: 'Although your order cannot be processed at this time, *we may be able to supply you with a generator on a temporary basis.*'
Words	Avoid 'hot button' words and euphemisms. Refer to groups or situations rather than individuals.

Table 2.9 (cont'd): techniques for conveying bad news

Voice	Use the passive rather than active voice to convey bad news (impersonal passive is best in some cases): 'Your request cannot be granted' rather than 'I cannot grant your request'.
Mood	Use subjunctive, rather than indicative or imperative: 'If you were able to…'

Table 2.10 (see pp. 39–41) lists a number of different approaches you can take when delivering bad news.

Let's now apply some of these ideas to a sample bad news letter. Letter A (figure 2.5 on p. 42) presents an ineffective bad news letter, in which the writer demonstrates aggression and insensitivity. Letter B (figure 2.6 on p. 43) illustrates the opposite, equally ineffective tendency — the writer is simply too passive, and in fact indiscreet. Both these extremes are of course exaggerated for effect; only a thoroughly incompetent writer would send out letters as bad as these. Letter C (figure 2.7 on pp. 44–45) presents a more effective bad news letter, in which many of the techniques we have considered are applied.

Table 2.10: approaches to bad news situations

Situation	Possible appreciation, restatement, agreement buffers	Possible explanation buffers	Possible expression of bad news	Possible alternatives
Credit refusal	'Thank you for choosing to shop at Hellier's'	'We feel that it is unfair and unwise to ask customers to commit more than 12 per cent of their income to account repayments'	'In these circumstances, we would be unable to offer you account facilities'	Offer lay-by/lay-away scheme Offer discount for cash payment Suggest customer reapply when financial situation improves
Loan refusal	'We agree that a reliable line of credit is extremely helpful for all start-up businesses'	'It would, of course, be unwise for you to over-commit yourself at this time, given the unstable nature of your market'	'We feel that it would be unwise to proceed at this time with the line of credit we have been discussing'	Offer smaller loan Suggest customer reapply when market situation improves
Adjustment	'Thank you for your letter and package of 4 September containing a returned copy of *Quill* software'	'The software envelope appears to have been opened and re-glued. Unfortunately this voids the *Quill* warranty and . . .'	'. . . your package is returned herewith'	Offer good trade-in/upgrade allowance Offer discount on future purchase Give information about other products

Table 2.10 *(cont'd)*: approaches to bad news situations

Situation	Possible appreciation, restatement, agreement buffers	Possible explanation buffers	Possible expression of bad news	Possible alternatives
Item not in stock	'Your order (18 January 2008) for twelve Waveform AA2 speakers shows you to be a true connoisseur of sound'	'Recent favourable publicity has caused a rush on our stocks, and we have had to increase production to meet orders'	'Your Waveform speakers will be delivered to you on the amended date of 4 October'	Promise a specific (amended) delivery date Offer reduced charges (for example, on delivery)
Item discontinued	'Your order (18 January 2008) for twelve Waveform speakers shows you to be a true connoisseur of sound'	'To meet our commitment to stay at the cutting edge of innovation, we have now produced the AA3 series, which supersedes the AA2 model . . .'	'. . . production of which has been discontinued'	Offer superior alternative or substitute on sale/loan/rental/lease Offer new product at old price Offer old product at old/reduced price (to clear stock) Offer smaller quantities of new product, so customer does not have to pay any more

Situation	Possible appreciation, restatement, agreement buffers	Possible explanation buffers	Possible expression of bad news	Possible alternatives
Price increase	'Thank you for being a long-term Waveform customer. Your commitment to excellence in sound allows us to do what we enjoy doing most—produce the world's top speaker systems'	'As a professional, you know that research and development and state-of-the-art materials don't come cheap. If you wanted the cheapies, you wouldn't be listening to Waveform!'	'Accordingly, Waveform prices will need to rise by 8 per cent as of 1 June (see attached list)'	Offer choice in terms of payment Mention other, cheaper alternative products/services/models/lines
Unsuccessful job application	'We are gratified that you were interested enough in DayCo to approach us'	'Your qualifications, experience and references, while impressive ...'	'... do not match our requirements at this time'	Suggest other possible employers Offer to keep application on file
Money solicited	'I admire the work you have done with homeless children and the non-English-speaking unemployed'	'We make large corporate donations each year to the Wider Community Benefit Fund ...'	'... and thus cannot provide you with a direct donation this financial year'	Mention other organisations (for example, general charities) to which money has been given and to which the solicitor could apply to

Figure 2.5: letter A, an ineffective bad news letter—too aggressive

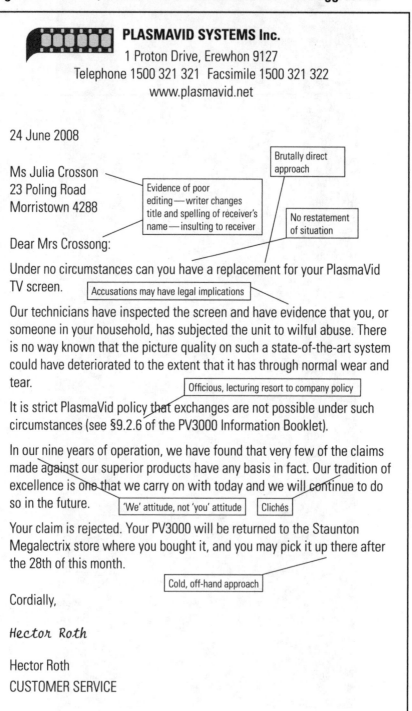

PLASMAVID SYSTEMS Inc.
1 Proton Drive, Erewhon 9127
Telephone 1500 321 321 Facsimile 1500 321 322
www.plasmavid.net

24 June 2008

Ms Julia Crosson
23 Poling Road
Morristown 4288

Dear Mrs Crossong:

> Brutally direct approach

> Evidence of poor editing—writer changes title and spelling of receiver's name—insulting to receiver

> No restatement of situation

Under no circumstances can you have a replacement for your PlasmaVid TV screen.

> Accusations may have legal implications

Our technicians have inspected the screen and have evidence that you, or someone in your household, has subjected the unit to wilful abuse. There is no way known that the picture quality on such a state-of-the-art system could have deteriorated to the extent that it has through normal wear and tear.

> Officious, lecturing resort to company policy

It is strict PlasmaVid policy that exchanges are not possible under such circumstances (see §9.2.6 of the PV3000 Information Booklet).

In our nine years of operation, we have found that very few of the claims made against our superior products have any basis in fact. Our tradition of excellence is one that we carry on with today and we will continue to do so in the future.

> 'We' attitude, not 'you' attitude

> Clichés

Your claim is rejected. Your PV3000 will be returned to the Staunton Megalectrix store where you bought it, and you may pick it up there after the 28th of this month.

> Cold, off-hand approach

Cordially,

Hector Roth

Hector Roth
CUSTOMER SERVICE

Figure 2.6: letter B, an ineffective bad news letter—too passive

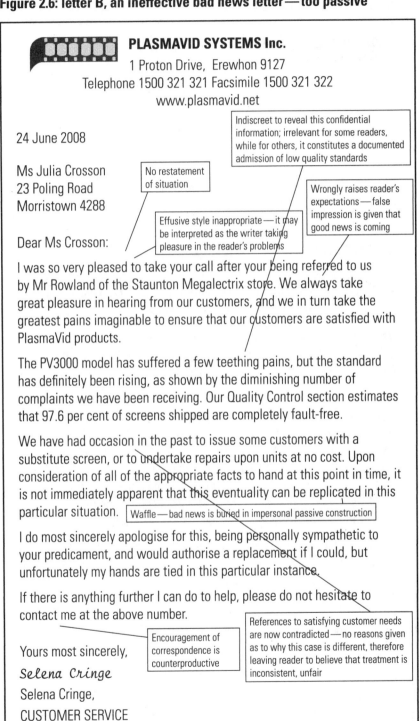

PLASMAVID SYSTEMS Inc.
1 Proton Drive, Erewhon 9127
Telephone 1500 321 321 Facsimile 1500 321 322
www.plasmavid.net

24 June 2008

Ms Julia Crosson
23 Poling Road
Morristown 4288

Dear Ms Crosson:

> No restatement of situation

> Indiscreet to reveal this confidential information; irrelevant for some readers, while for others, it constitutes a documented admission of low quality standards

> Wrongly raises reader's expectations—false impression is given that good news is coming

> Effusive style inappropriate—it may be interpreted as the writer taking pleasure in the reader's problems

I was so very pleased to take your call after your being referred to us by Mr Rowland of the Staunton Megalectrix store. We always take great pleasure in hearing from our customers, and we in turn take the greatest pains imaginable to ensure that our customers are satisfied with PlasmaVid products.

The PV3000 model has suffered a few teething pains, but the standard has definitely been rising, as shown by the diminishing number of complaints we have been receiving. Our Quality Control section estimates that 97.6 per cent of screens shipped are completely fault-free.

We have had occasion in the past to issue some customers with a substitute screen, or to undertake repairs upon units at no cost. Upon consideration of all of the appropriate facts to hand at this point in time, it is not immediately apparent that this eventuality can be replicated in this particular situation.

> Waffle—bad news is buried in impersonal passive construction

I do most sincerely apologise for this, being personally sympathetic to your predicament, and would authorise a replacement if I could, but unfortunately my hands are tied in this particular instance.

If there is anything further I can do to help, please do not hesitate to contact me at the above number.

> References to satisfying customer needs are now contradicted—no reasons given as to why this case is different, therefore leaving reader to believe that treatment is inconsistent, unfair

Yours most sincerely,

> Encouragement of correspondence is counterproductive

Selena Cringe

Selena Cringe,
CUSTOMER SERVICE

Figure 2.7: letter C, an effective bad news letter

PLASMAVID SYSTEMS Inc.
1 Proton Drive, Erewhon 9127
Telephone 1500 321 321 Facsimile 1500 321 322
www.plasmavid.net

24 June 2008

> Statement of commitment, linked to description of procedures, which form basis of explanation

> Explanation based on verifiable fact, therefore limiting scope of customer to dispute the decision

Ms Julia Crosson
23 Poling Road
Morristown 4288

> Appreciation buffer. Restatement of details of situation show personal touch

Dear Ms Crosson:

> Passive voice, de-emphasising blame of customer and decision of writer

Thank you for taking the trouble to return your PV3000 television unit to the Staunton Megalectrix store. Mr John Rowland of Megalectrix has conveyed your views to me via email and telephone.

We are always concerned when one of our products does not meet the requirements of our customers, and automatically subject any returned items to stringent laboratory tests.

On this occasion, it was discovered that the back seals have been breached, and the central input unit appears to have been removed, subjected to strong distorting impact pressure, and reinserted into the custom plug array with pressure that has led to the yellow pickup pins being bent. This type of damage is sometimes seen when unauthorised attempts are made to insert illegal game console emulation chips and illegal cable programming chips. I attach a copy of the report, incorporating digital photographs used in the inspection.

The PlasmaVid Warranty does not cover such circumstances, and thus it is not possible to issue a full refund on the price or to provide another model free of charge.

> Options are offered

I can, however, offer you a number of options:

1 Expert factory repair of plug/pin unit (cost $154)

2 A voucher (valid at any store) which will guarantee you a trade-in price of $5050 on a new PV3000 (recommended retail price: $8555) or an approved second-hand PlasmaVid product.

Please telephone me at 1500 321 916 (direct) and advise me how we can best help you.

Yours sincerely,

Jane Carruthers

Jane Carruthers
CUSTOMER SERVICE

> Puts ball back in court of customer. Offer of contact with writer may be risky—customer may wish to drag out dispute—but objective proof of damage will lessen the likelihood of this

Encs.

Try it yourself

1. Assume that you are the manager of a sporting goods store. While reviewing your monthly accounts, you find that twenty-four of your customers have been wrongly charged an $18 accounting fee. Write a standard letter, telling them the good news of their refund.

2. Assume that you work in the shareholder communications branch of Gigabank. Gigabank has performed well this year, so shareholders will receive a record dividend of 12 per cent and a bonus of 2 per cent. Write a good news letter that can be signed by the general manager. This letter will become a template for all such communications mailed out with dividend payments.

3. You work in the marketing department at Duplic8 photocopiers. The new Omega model is meant to be shipped to retailers on 1 September, but this isn't going to happen. Unexpected materials shortages, problems in quality testing and general all-round bungling have seen to that. Your manager has asked you to draft a form letter to retailers, announcing that the launch will be delayed by three weeks. Write the letter, inventing whatever details you feel are necessary.

Try it yourself *(cont'd)*

4   You are the human resources manager at DayCo manufacturing. An
    old friend, Celia Higgins, has asked you to accept a late application
    for a management-trainee position from her daughter, Christine.
    Christine's application was poorly presented, and while her
    qualifications were just acceptable, she has had little experience
    in the requisite areas. Write her a letter advising her that she did not
    get the position. Invent whatever details you feel
    are necessary.

Letters 3 — persuading

In chapter 2, approaches to writing letters in good news situations (the reader will be pleased to read what you write) and bad news situations (where the reader will probably not be very happy with what you write) were explored. Chapter 3 deals with situations where writers want to persuade their readers of something. You may recognise some of these approaches as those that are used by writers of 'junk mail'. However, the approach here will not be the crass hard-sell of junk mail but the subtle and discerning one of ethical persuasion.

Persuasive letters

Letters are one of the most important channels used to persuade others. The following are some techniques that writers employ to persuade their readers.

Structuring persuasive documents: the AIDA sequence

A useful way of structuring persuasive documents is to apply the *AIDA sequence* (for attention, interest, desire, action) as shown in figure 3.1. Contrast the AIDA model with the MADE model (message, action, details, evidence) for emails on page 114.

Figure 3.1: the AIDA sequence in structuring persuasive documents

OCEAN VIEW ESTATE INC.
44 Vista Boulevard, Ocean View 41920
Phone 1800 321 321 Facsimile 1800 322 322
Email info@oceanviewnow.net
Internet www.oceanviewnow.net

Dear_____

As you will know, housing has never been less affordable. Today you could face a debt load three times of the one that your parents took on just for a roof over your head!

But don't despair — Ocean View Estate on the north coast is based on a new release of government land, at zero cost to you. Power, gas, water, sewerage and data/TV cabling have been provided at no cost by the state government, and there's a 35-minute, high-speed rail link to the city centre. Best of all, our new sustainable energy house models are priced from an ultra-low $79,999!

You'll love the price, the ocean view and the fresh air. You'll save heaps, live the life of a millionaire, and be in touch with the heart of the city.

For a free brochure showing everything Ocean View Estate has to offer, call 1800 321 321 now, or visit our website at www.oceanviewnow.net.

1 Get attention
2 Stimulate interest
3 Create desire
4 Elicit action

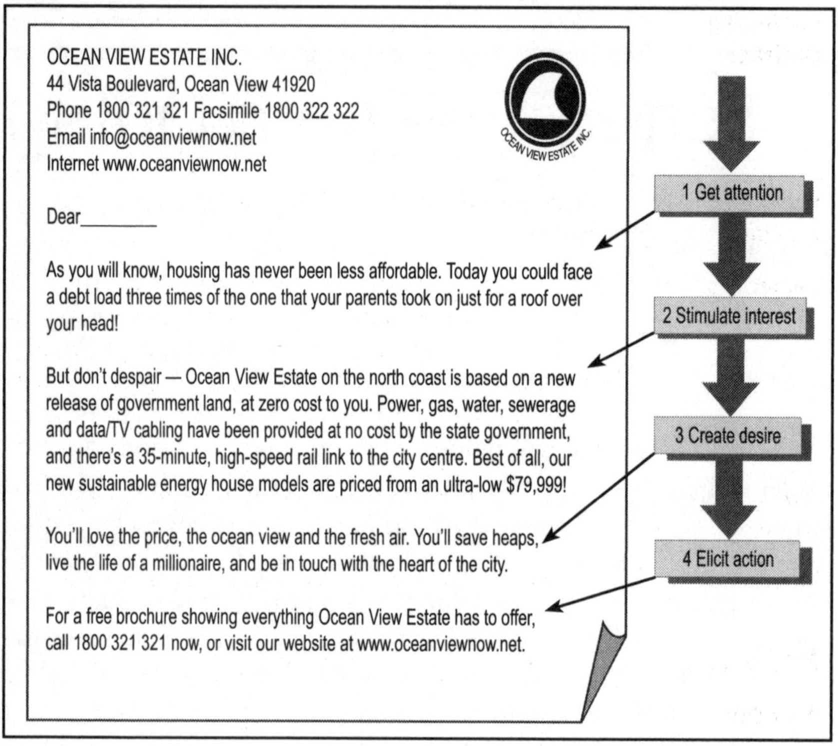

Getting attention

Persuasive communications can be either solicited or unsolicited. A solicited communication is one requested by the receiver—there has been prior communication between sender and receiver (perhaps a telephone call). In solicited communications, there is no need to grab the attention of the reader or audience (although it should never be taken for granted).

In unsolicited persuasive communications (for example, a sales letter), it is essential to grab the attention of the reader or audience right away. Readers of unsolicited communications often make up their minds very quickly, sometimes too quickly. First impressions are often final impressions. Table 3.1 lists some of the ways this all-important initial interest may be sought.

Table 3.1: ways of attracting reader interest

Interesting statistics	'Most of our staff admit to losing at least forty minutes a day handling junk emails, wrong telephone numbers and telemarketers, and redirecting customers. If we could free up that time, that's the equivalent of getting a thirteenth or bonus month of productivity each year.'
Rhetorical question	'Would you like to make $5000 tax free in the next three months?'
Quotations	'Isn't it better to have men being ungrateful than to miss a chance to do good?' (Denis Diderot, 18th-century French philosopher). Many of us are sceptical about giving to charity because we feel that it doesn't do any good, but have you ever thought that the greatest beneficiary of giving is yourself, and your own peace of mind?'
Unusual facts	'The average person will spend four years of their lives watching television commercials.'
Humour	'Did you know that income tax has made more liars out of people than fishing and golf combined?'
Pointed questions	'Will you have enough money to retire on?'
Anecdote	'A young man started a magazine in 1956, selling only thirty-two copies of the first issue. That magazine now sells over 1.2 million copies per issue in the Asia–Pacific region alone.'

Stimulating interest

Having gained the reader's attention, the next task is to create an interest in, and a desire for, the product, process or idea. Features (or characteristics) and proofs (for instance, statistics, samples, guarantees) are critical here. By stressing features and proofs, you hope to be able to engage the logical decision-making faculties of your reader.

Creating desire

We don't always make decisions with the head only, often we are guided by the heart and by our own self-interest. To create desire in the reader or audience we need to keep the 'you' attitude in mind, addressing the question 'What's in it for you?' We can answer this question by stressing the benefits as distinct from features, and by tapping into the motivational patterns of our reader or audience.

Elicit action

Once the reader's attention has been gained, and interest and desire stimulated, it is necessary to elicit an action response. Action can be stimulated by making a response easy for the reader. Such stimulants include:

- enclosing prepaid envelopes
- enclosing reply-paid forms that are simple to complete
- giving toll-free telephone and fax numbers
- allowing payment by credit card
- offering deferred payment ('send nothing now — we'll bill you later').

Proofs such as guarantees, samples and trial periods should be mentioned now if they have not already been covered in the interest and desire sections of the document. Incentives for prompt response may include discounts, free entry in a lottery or gifts. Postscript messages at the end of such letters are, perhaps surprisingly, the most often read part of some sales letters.

Message plus ...

The overall appearance of the persuasive message can be vital to its reception, as can the presence of other material enclosed with the message. Letterheads, embossing, the quality and colour of paper used in envelopes and letters — all of these can convey powerful non-verbal messages to the reader. Ensure that they are positive messages rather than negative ones.

Various items can be enclosed with your primary document. The most common of these is a brochure of some kind. A brochure or similar document 'takes the pressure off' the main document—the writer does not have to cram all of the information into a single text letter and can simply refer the reader to appropriate sections of the brochure. Most readers will not read the full message anyway but will skim and scan, while their eye will be drawn to an attractive detail in a colour brochure.

Other enclosures include proofs (such as samples) and gifts. Pens, rulers, mouse pads and other inexpensive gifts, suitably inscribed with logos and other advertising devices, may well outlast kilos of paper communications, and may eventually get your message across by dint of pure physical survival.

Other types of persuasion—complaint, claims and collections

Persuasion involves efforts to 'sell' products, processes or ideas. Let's consider some very different situations that arise after such persuasion has been successful—sometimes too successful.

Collection letters

Collection letters are sent when purchasers are late with payment. Normally sent by organisations to individuals or other organisations, the writer has two objectives:

1   to secure the money owed

2   to preserve the goodwill and reputation of both parties.

Why not simply send a debtor a one-line letter reading 'Pay up or else?' as soon as a bill or invoice is overdue? This would be ill-advised, for a number of reasons:

- It's illegal to make threats.

- It's unethical.

- It's insensitive—there may be very good reasons why payment has not been forthcoming.

- It may be counterproductive, evoking an aggressive and hostile response from recipients, making them even less likely to pay.

- It may have significant negative public relations payoffs. If the collection process is handled sensitively, the recipients' goodwill will be retained (it may even be strengthened), and they may relay positive word-of-mouth perceptions about the sender through their personal networks. If the collection process is handled badly, the recipients' goodwill will be lost, and negative perceptions of the sender may be passed on through the recipients' personal networks.

Writers of collection letters normally calibrate their messages to reflect the urgency of different situations. As the period of non-payment becomes longer, collection letters become progressively less indirect and more direct—less about persuasion and more about demand.

Typically, collection letters are created in response to three or four different phases or situations (see table 3.2 on p. 54). Each of these phases lasts fourteen or thirty days. Letters may be accompanied and reinforced by telephone calls and, on occasion, personal meetings.

Phase one: reminder

A reminder is sent out on the assumption that the recipient has merely overlooked the payment. This assumption is often correct, and sometimes the reminder letter will cross the payment in the mail.

Phase two: enquiry

In this phase the writer no longer assumes oversight on the part of the debtor, but rather infers that special circumstances are creating a legitimate barrier to payment. The benefit of the doubt is extended to the debtor, giving him or her an opportunity to rectify the situation—either through full payment or via a negotiated schedule of part-payments. When writing collection letters, enquire about the recipient's circumstances, but don't ask whether the product/process was unsatisfactory. This risks simply prolonging matters.

Phase three: appeal

If there is still no reply, matters proceed to phase three. Up until now positive approaches have been tried (empathy, concern, problem solving). Now it is time to introduce greater resolution. The writer may try a number of appeals to the reader.

The first appeal may be to equity or fair play: the recipient has benefited by using the product or process—surely it's only ethical that he or she pay for it. Another appeal may be to fear—vague or oblique references may be made to legal action. A third appeal may be to a mixture of pride, fear and self-interest—the recipient's hard-won credit rating may be damaged.

Phase four: ultimatum

Having exhausted all other options, the writer is now no longer requesting but demanding action by the debtor. Specific consequences of continued dereliction need to be spelt out, along with deadlines. For example, unless payment is received in a nominated number of days, the account will be turned over to a collection agency ('we're not nasty, but they are'). The writer must be careful not to overstep the mark legally in any collection letter, but should be particularly careful with ultimatum or final demand letters—know what you can legally demand and go no further. If necessary, seek legal advice.

Ultimatum letters are given additional weight by being sent by special mail or being signed by someone more senior in the organisation than the writer of the previous letters. If possible, hold out some hope that the damage can be undone if payment is made—this is not only ethical and pragmatic, but sound public relations too. Some organisations only go through the motions with letters of this kind, preferring to write off a relatively small proportion of bad debts rather than risk negative public relations impacts.

Table 3.2 (overleaf) lists the different types of collection letters, their approach and sample wording.

Table 3.2: different types of collection letters

Phase	Phase name	Days overdue	Approach	Sample wording
1	Reminder	30	Indirect approach Assumption: simple misunderstanding, oversight	'We appreciate your custom, and attach details of next week's sale.' 'We understand it is often easy to overlook payments of accounts in today's busy world. Please attend to the attached bill in order to avoid unnecessary interest payments.'
2	Enquiry	60	Indirect approach Assumption of misunderstanding dropped. New assumption — there is a legitimate reason preventing payment	'We note that this account has not been paid for some time. Is there something wrong? If you are experiencing difficulties meeting this payment, please contact us and we can discuss other payment options.'
3	Appeal	90	More direct approach Assumption: there is a growing danger of complete default Appeals to equity/ fair play, pride, fear, self-interest	'You have built up a good reputation as a reliable customer of ours over a number of years. We would be sorry to see that reputation suffer, and your credit rating along with it. Please attend to this outstanding payment as soon as possible.'
4	Ultimatum	120	Direct approach Assumption: preservation of goodwill is still important, but getting payment is now paramount	'If we have not received your payment of $495.95 by 11 June, we will have to place this matter with the Implacable Debt Collection agency.'

Try it yourself

1   Assume that you are the general manager of a new branch of the community bank VillageBank. You are overseeing the fitting out of the office space on the main street of the suburb of Eastleigh. You have ample supplies of VillageBank brochures but decide to do a mail-out of letters to every household in a five-kilometre radius of the bank. VillageBank head office has purchased the mailing list database for you from a commercial service and is interested in seeing whether a local mail campaign will have any impact on customer growth. The major banks have created much ill feeling in the past few years by increasing existing fees and creating new ones for personal and business customers. They have also alienated many of their older customers by forcing the pace on inducing people to use automatic tellers and internet banking. Write a letter to each household and business in your target area endeavouring to persuade them to set up at least one new account at the VillageBank branch or to consider taking out a loan for personal, housing or business purposes.

2   You are the finance manager of Green Energy, a company that specialises in generating and selling sustainable power to domestic and business customers. You notice that a number of your corporate clients have overdue bills. Write a series of collection letters that can be used as templates by your staff in extracting payment from these corporate clients.

Chapter 4

Memos

It's time to turn your attention from one paper-based format or genre—the letter—to another: the memo.

Memos

Most letters are sent to recipients outside the writer's organisation. Memos, or memorandums (from the Latin *memorandus*: to be remembered), are usually transmitted within an organisation. Memos may be created on paper or sent as emails.

Examples of a typical letter and a typical memo, highlighting the differences between the two forms of documents, are shown in figures 4.1 (pp. 58–59) and 4.2 (pp. 59–60).

Figure 4.1: letter format and style

JUGGERNAUT MANUFACTURING INC.

1000 Eastmore Road, Newtown 68113 Freedonia
Telephone (612) 419 6911 Toll-free (612) 008 420 4322
Facsimile (612) 419 6924
www.juggernautfacture.com

Full address details

11 September 2008

Ms Joanne Ajogalu,
Production Manager,
Close Shaves Company,
11 West Place,
Tiriel Industrial Park 91233

Full name, title, address of reader

Dear Ms Ajogalu:

Salutation

<u>Ceramic Razor Blade Strip</u>

Following our phone conversations, I am writing to you to apologise for the non-delivery of your order of 40 × 80 kg reels of 3 mm ceramic razor blade strip. Delivery will now occur on 18 June at 9.30 am at your No. 3 Bay.

The volatility of production of new materials such as ceramic strip is notorious, but we at Juggernaut and Close Shaves entered into this production mode with our eyes open, because we both believe in the product's ability to ultimately give Close Shaves a market advantage over other companies using conventional metal strip.

We are satisfied the problems with the thermoelectric kilns have now been eliminated, and would be happy to have Mr Percy and his quality people from Close Shave drop over at any time to confirm this.

As I mentioned in our conversation, Juggernaut's plastics division may be able to provide you with a better product, both in terms of price and quality, than your current suppliers. If we were able to supply both the razor strip and the plastic handles for your razors, I am sure that Shane DiMeola of our plastics division and I could make the total pricing package even more attractive.

Formal style

Please take this up with your management group, as discussed, and get back to me. Should you require any further information, please call me direct on 419 6111.

Yours sincerely,

Brian McLeod ——— Signature

Brian McLeod, ——— Writer's name at end
Chief Executive Officer,
Ceramics Division

BMcL: lh

Figure 4.2: memo format and style

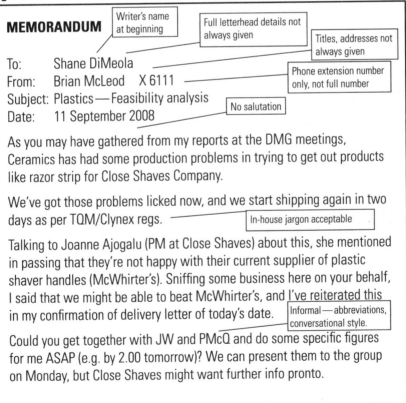

MEMORANDUM — Writer's name at beginning

Full letterhead details not always given

Titles, addresses not always given

To: Shane DiMeola
From: Brian McLeod   X 6111 — Phone extension number only, not full number
Subject: Plastics—Feasibility analysis
Date: 11 September 2008 — No salutation

As you may have gathered from my reports at the DMG meetings, Ceramics has had some production problems in trying to get out products like razor strip for Close Shaves Company.

We've got those problems licked now, and we start shipping again in two days as per TQM/Clynex regs. — In-house jargon acceptable

Talking to Joanne Ajogalu (PM at Close Shaves) about this, she mentioned in passing that they're not happy with their current supplier of plastic shaver handles (McWhirter's). Sniffing some business here on your behalf, I said that we might be able to beat McWhirter's, and I've reiterated this in my confirmation of delivery letter of today's date. — Informal—abbreviations, conversational style.

Could you get together with JW and PMcQ and do some specific figures for me ASAP (e.g. by 2.00 tomorrow)? We can present them to the group on Monday, but Close Shaves might want further info pronto.

Figure 4.2 *(cont'd)*: memo format and style

We'd need to know:

1. capacity/cost data for bulk plastic (Close Shaves do their own stamping of handles—pick up samples of shavers from RT in my office)

2. capacity/cost data (including prototyping, rejigging, moulds, floor space) if we do it for them.

Big heretical thought for all—what if we ditch Close Shaves and do the whole thing ourselves, through a new retail operation? Too much trouble? Or bold new move? I'll put it on the agenda.

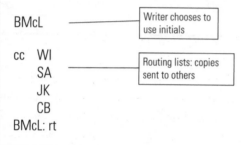

BMcL — Writer chooses to use initials

cc WI — Routing lists: copies sent to others
    SA
    JK
    CB
BMcL: rt

What are memos for?

Don't send memos when face-to-face or telephone interaction will solve your communication problem more quickly and directly. Nevertheless, if there is a case for putting it in writing, do so. Bear in mind that everything we have considered about letters in terms of general communication principles still holds true—memo recipients, like letter recipients, have basic needs for information and respect.

A memorandum is written not to inform the reader but to protect the writer.
Dean Acheson

Many types of memos are used in organisations. Let's consider four:

- request memos

- announcement memos

- instruction memos

- warning memos.

Request memos

Request memos are a common form of written communication. Such memos go beyond information-only documents—the writer expects the recipient to take action, and to communicate that action either in person, by telephone or via another memo. This type of document carries a strong element of accountability. An example of a request memo is shown in figure 4.2.

Announcement memos

Announcement memos usually have large audiences. Rather than being addressed to one person, perhaps with copies to several others, announcement memos are addressed to, say, a group, a department or the whole organisation. The interests of everyone are affected by the content of the memo, and it is therefore more efficient to send out a single, duplicated memo than to personalise it many times over. Such memos may be sent through internal paper mail, displayed on noticeboards or sent as emails.

Layout is perhaps of more importance in announcement memos than in other types of memos, as people may not scan a publicly displayed memo with the care they would give to one they have received personally. Thoughtful composition and design involving different fonts, subheadings or bulleted lists will help this type of memo communicate effectively. Announcement memos are information-only documents—readers are usually not expected to respond directly (see figure 4.3 overleaf).

Instruction memos

An *instruction memo* sets out information about procedures or operating routines. Like announcement memos, they tend to be given broadcast distribution, and a reply from recipients is not normally expected.

Writing instructions, procedures or policy is not necessarily as easy as it looks. These memos place a heavy emphasis on facts, sequences and covering all possibilities and options (see figure 4.4). If writing, for example, on how to operate a machine or system, it is important that a logical sequence be followed, without assuming that certain intermediate steps are so obvious that such details can be omitted.

Instruction memos are sometimes issued when procedures in a certain area have become so complex that commonsense understandings are no longer adequate. They may also be issued to neutralise controversies over scarce resources, or the misuse of facilities and equipment.

Figure 4.3: an announcement memo

 **CLONE POWER**

Suite 39, Rintrah Industrial Park, Claymore 23121 Freedonia
Telephone (615) 1233 4352 Facsimile (615) 1233 4378
www.clonepower.com Customer service info@clonepower.com

To: All Staff	Subject: Compulsory Superannuation — Salary Deductions
From: Priscilla Khan	Date: 5 September 2007

There has been much discussion in the media about the federal government's proposal to make superannuation compulsory for all employees.

If this proposal is implemented, deductions will start at 5 per cent of salary, and increase to 8 per cent over a period of five years.

There will be briefing sessions on this proposal for all staff on Monday, 12 February.

TIMES:	Every hour, on the hour, from 9.00 am to 9.00 pm (All three shifts should therefore be able to attend)
DURATION:	Approximately 30 minutes
VENUE:	Conference Room B

SUPERVISORS: Please ensure that all personnel in your area have a chance to attend a session.

A video will be made of one of the sessions and will be available for viewing in the Training Centre from 9.00 am, Tuesday 13 September.

Figure 4.4: an instruction memo

GONDWANA CONSULTING INC.
44 Bay Road, Utopia 9210
www.gondwana.com

TO: ALL STAFF	FROM: NATALIE BSWANA
SUBJECT: CAR POOL PROCEDURE	DATE: 22 November 2009

Following are the new procedures for use of company vehicles.

1   All vehicles need to be booked at least eight hours in advance of when needed. This can be done by:

- booking via the intranet site
- phoning Facilities on x178
- sending a print memo.

2   All vehicle logbooks must be updated. Record speedometer figures for the beginning of your journey and for its completion.

3   Any accidents or incidents of any kind should be reported to the Fleet Supervisor immediately on return to base. If involved in an accident or incident, you will also have to complete a D19 form.

4   All vehicles are kept fully fuelled from supplies on base. Should you require additional fuel, you can either:

- pay for fuel personally and present a receipt to the Fleet Supervisor so that you can be reimbursed
- pay for fuel on a company card (if you have one). If you do this, email Fran in accounts <fran@central.gondwana.com> with the details so she can reconcile amounts on monthly card statements.

5   No vehicle is to be used for personal use unless your area coordinator advises the fleet supervisor by phone, memo or email.

Warning memos

The *warning memo* is concerned with the dark side of organisational life. Warning memos are sent when there is a perception that someone is not doing the right thing. The warning may be low-key and confidential, with perhaps no copy going to anyone else. This is the type of communication that might be written if a writer thought that verbal hints or warnings were not hitting their mark by changing the behaviour of the target person. As the gravity of the warning increases, the likelihood of copies being sent to others increases. In the first instance, however, the warning memo may be sent in hard copy only, as a paper document. That is the whole point of the exercise—to maintain confidentiality, by using a paper document only, but with the message conveying a threat that other channels will be used if this one doesn't work.

Warning memos may form part of a formal discipline procedure, perhaps leading to dismissal or termination. Care has to be taken in the wording of warning memos, primarily due not just to the feelings of the target person, but also because if the content is not factually incontrovertible, then there may be legal repercussions (see figure 4.5). Do not make accusations you cannot substantiate, and do not use abusive or demeaning language. While there is still hope of a negative situation being turned around, try and accentuate any positives there are.

Figure 4.5: a warning memo

To: Mitch Presbury, Welfare Clients/North Zone Management Team
From: Zach Warrell, Welfare Clients Division Manager
Subject: Download Problems
Date: 19 September 2007

Further to our brief conversation today, I thought it useful to document my views on this situation.

An IT professional like yourself knows the cost involved in running a corporate broadband service, and is also aware of company policy on downloading personal and/or offensive material.

Despite your protestations that neither you nor anyone in your department is involved in inappropriate use of the system, the new security tracking software I have been using suggests otherwise, as do total download figures for the past two months.

You are responsible for usage in your area, just as I am responsible for usage in the broader division. We are presumed by head office to be completely in control of electronic traffic and that extends to legal liability as well. As I mentioned to you in our conversation, recent local and interstate legal actions involving the downloading of inappropriate material (games, pornography, etc.) demonstrate that we all need to be vigilant in this regard.

This memo has not been copied to anyone, and I see no need for this matter to proceed any further right now. However, if I do become aware of further problems arising in this area, I will send you an email or paper memo as a formal warning with copies to HK and BLJ in head office, with a date-stamped copy of this memo attached.

You are a skilled person, Mitch, and we do not want to lose such skills if it can be helped. Let's work together on this, and not against each other.

Try it yourself

1   You have been assigned the duty of running the annual Christmas party in an organisation you are familiar with. Write an announcement memo to all staff, setting out details of time, venue, entertainment, costs and any other details you feel are relevant.

2   You are the general manager of welfare services at the local council. You supervise 322 staff, who run five different child day-care, disabled industry training and aged-care facilities. Last year two highly favourable articles were written in national newspapers about your operations, and the articles have since been reproduced overseas.

You have just been notified that a delegation of federal politicians and overseas journalists will be visiting your offices in three weeks' time. You decide to organise a team presentation about all the operations in your areas. Send out a request memo to all five facilities' team leaders, asking for current information about their operations. What case study material can they provide? What visual content (diagrams, digital photographs) could be used in the presentation? Invent whatever details you need.

3   Consider something (an item of equipment, a software package, a recipe) you are familiar with. Write an instruction memo to another person, real or fictitious, on how to use it.

4   Assume you are the head of sales at Juggernaut Manufacturing. Angela Hayes, one of your best sales representatives, has arrived smelling of alcohol several times in the past week, and apparently affected by her alcohol intake. You have attempted to raise the matter in a half-joking way, but Angela has taken offence at your remarks. She is a competent professional, in fact one of your rising stars, but you cannot ignore the situation in case it worsens. You spoke with her today in the corridor, trying to strike a more serious note, but she dismissed your concerns, affirming that her private life was hers and hers alone. You know that she has been involved in two minor accidents in the car park in the past fortnight, and graffiti about her condition is now appearing in both the male and female toilets on the floor you both work on. Write a warning memo to Angela.

Chapter 5

Reports

Earlier I looked at two shorter formats or genres—the letter and the memo. In this chapter I'm going to analyse a genre that is often longer in word count and scope—the report.

So you've got to write a report...

Writing a report, particularly a long report, is a bit like going to the dentist—no-one likes doing it, but it's got to be done. You can, however, make that perception work for you. If you are one of the few people—perhaps the only person—in your organisation who can write a report, and write a good report, it will do your career profile no damage at all—quite the contrary. Being known as a good report writer means that you are competent at describing and analysing situations and people.

Reports can be just a few words long or can extend to multiple bound volumes. They can deal with routine or non-routine matters. The writer may have to make all decisions relating to content, layout and design, or the format may be preset, with the writer needing only to feed in a few new figures and updates. Most reports are still paper-based, although an increasing number are completed and submitted online.

There are many types of reports, as set out in table 5.1. In this chapter, however, I will focus primarily on analytical, or research, reports. I will also consider some types of documents that bear a strong resemblance to reports—namely, submissions, proposals or tenders.

People don't read today; they flip.
John Lyon

Table 5.1: some report/proposal formats

Report type	Function	Audience	Format and features
Computer or data report	Gives quick visual overview of data	Mainly internal Decision-makers and process monitors	Mainly graphic renditions of tabular data from databases and spreadsheets Minimal amount of descriptive and analytical text Often created with specialised software (e.g. Crystal Reports) Rarely involves conclusions or recommendations
Incident report	Gives quick overview of event not associated with human injury	Mainly internal Decision-makers and process monitors	Strongly fact-based—what, where, why, who, when, how Created to document non-routine situation May be used to detect emerging problems May use standard format print/online document Occasionally will give conclusions and recommendations

Report type	Function	Audience	Format and features
Accident report	Gives quick overview of event associated with human injury	Mainly internal Decision-makers and process monitors	Strongly fact-based—what, where, why, who, when, how Created to document non-routine situation May be used to detect emerging problems May use standard format print/ online document Occasionally will give conclusions and recommendations Critical part of occupational health and safety/legal regimes
Periodic report	Gives quick picture of routine processes and situations	Mainly internal Decision-makers and process monitors	Documents routine situations Standardised format is used across time and space to facilitate comparability and monitoring Does not include conclusions or recommendations
Progress report	Gives picture of non-routine processes and situations	Mainly internal, but can be external, such as for clients Decision-makers and process monitors	Documents non-routine situations, such as projects Key function is to inform whether project is on schedule, and if not, why not Sometimes has standardised format May give conclusions and recommendations
Memo report	Gives picture of non-routine processes and situations	Mainly internal Decision-makers and process monitors	Longer than a standard memo More structured than a standard memo—will have sections with headings May involve conclusions and recommendations

Table 5.1 *(cont'd)*: some report/proposal formats

Report type	Function	Audience	Format and features
Letter report	Gives picture of non-routine processes and situations	Mainly external Decision-makers	Longer than a standard letter More structured than a standard letter—will have sections with headings May involve conclusions and recommendations
Justification report	Presents a case for change (e.g. a purchase, a new system and/or staffing)	Mainly internal Decision-makers	Needs to establish a rationale for change in status quo Case needs to be established based on research, costings Will involve conclusions and recommendations In effect, a short proposal
Accountability report	Gives quick picture of routine processes and situations	Mainly external Regulators, often in public sector	Examples include tax reports, environment/equal opportunity/health and safety/industry compliance documentation Usually on a periodic basis May use standard format print/online document Rarely gives conclusions and recommendations
Research or analytical report	Gives detailed analysis of a situation	Mainly internal Decision-makers	May be long (1000+ words) May involve considerable research Involves analysis as well as description Format and structure are created by writer, usually in accordance with conventions Will give conclusions and (usually) recommendations
Proposal/submission/tender	Presents a case for change (e.g. a purchase, a new system and/or staffing)	Can be internal or external Decision-makers	Similar in many respects to analytical report Used in competitive bidding situations

Report type	Function	Audience	Format and features
Annual report	Gives account of year's operation of organisation	Mainly external— shareholders and stakeholders Staff	May be elaborately designed, with high production values Meets legal requirements for accountability May not include any conclusions or recommendations

Information and persuasion—getting the mix right

The purpose of some report types is purely to provide specific information to their audience—just the facts, and nothing else. Others are intended to be persuasive—their object is to convince decision-makers, for example, to adopt a course of action or to buy a new piece of equipment. Figure 5.1 shows how different document types can be placed on a continuum, according to the information–persuasion mix. Does this mean that some documents are purely persuasive, while others are exclusively informative? Not necessarily. A persuasive document needs to contain proof as a basis for persuasion, while even the most basic informative document—for example, a simple report showing a graphic rendering of data from a spreadsheet—may prove more persuasive than a long but unconvincing and poorly presented analytical report on the same topic.

Figure 5.1: the information–persuasion continuum

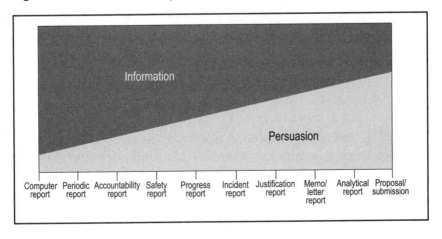

It follows, then, that while report writers can often get away with filling in a few boxes in routine report documents, they may need to become more versatile in order to create non-routine reports based on a synthesis of fact and opinion. Indeed, the more we progress in our careers, the more we will be required to produce documents dealing with non-routine situations.

Information, persuasion, entertainment, talk and lobbying

It's very important to get the information–persuasion mix of documents as balanced as possible. To be really effective, three other factors must also be considered.

First, consider the *look* of the document. Although reports are work-based documents, most of their readers will still appreciate a striking-looking, colourful design rather than a conventional, unimaginative black-and-white one. You don't have to be a trained graphic designer to recognise that a well designed, attractively presented document is likely to communicate a message more effectively.

Second, bear in mind that sometimes a written document marks the beginning of a communication process rather than the end. Increasingly, document writers are asked to give a spoken presentation—in effect, an oral report—to back up, or sometimes substitute, a written report. Software suites containing word processing and presentation programs make this task a lot easier (although sometimes it still makes sense to seek the help of a professional graphic designer). Be prepared, therefore, to deliver your report verbally as well as in writing. In some circumstances, your audience may not read a word of what you have written unless a spoken presentation from you piques their interest.

Finally, think about the extent to which the communication process reaches beyond the delivery of written and oral reports. Neither guarantees that your message is conveyed. Sometimes you need to lobby or attempt to influence members of your audience so that they will act on your recommendations. In other words, you have to write it, pitch it and sell it.

The big leap—writing essays and writing reports

Shortly I will examine techniques of report writing, but first I'd like to take a brief detour to look at some of the problems writers new to reports sometimes encounter.

The report is a specific genre of writing, like the novel, poetry, email or journalism. Within the report genre are sub-genres, such as memo reports and research reports. When asked to prepare a report for the first time, many writers draw inspiration from the genre they have had most experience with in their formal education—the essay. An essay is a document type that is concerned primarily with analysis rather than problem solving, and therefore rarely contains recommendations. Essay writing requires a complete set of skills, but many of these skills are different from those required for writing reports. The most common complaint about reports written by inexperienced writers is that they 'read like an essay, not a report'. Study the similarities and differences between the two genres in table 5.2, and respect them.

Table 5.2: reports and essays compared

Genre	Essay	Report
Approach	Tends to concentrate on analysis of a situation or problem, without necessarily providing solutions	Tends to be problem-focused and action-oriented
Topic/focus	Usually set by others as topic to be answered	Usually set by others as a brief or terms of reference
Table of contents	Not often included	Common in longer documents
Context	Academic world—submitted for marks; one of many submitted	World of work—submitted to aid decision making and problem solving, but will attract compliments, criticism or both; usually only one submitted
Summary	Not often included	Usually given, often mentioning key conclusions and recommendations

Table 5.2 *(cont'd)*: reports and essays compared

Genre	Essay	Report
Audience reading style	Likely to read all the way through; unlikely to reread	Likely to skim; may reread for reference
Introduction	Usually included; sets scene for what is to come	Always included; sets scene for what is to come
Discussion/ analysis	Yes — the main body of writing	Yes — the main body of writing
Conclusion	Yes — sums up the situation, gives an overview	Yes — sums up the situation, gives an overview
Recommendations	Not usually made	Usually made — suggest specific course of action that report reader may choose to take
Layout techniques	Paragraphs tend to be longer Sections and subsections not often numbered Bullet points not often used	Paragraphs tend to be shorter Sections and subsections often numbered, giving clear signposts to structure Bullet points sometimes used
Tables, graphics	Not always used	Often used to show data
Expression of opinion	Opinions are often expressed throughout	Opinions tend to be reserved for conclusions and recommendations
Style	May be impersonal and objective, or personal and subjective	Tends to be objective and impersonal
Referencing, quotation	May be extensive; secondary data tends to predominate	Usually light; primary data may be used as much as secondary data
Authoring	Usually individual	Often collective
Relationship to spoken presentation	Does not often lead to spoken presentation	Can often lead to oral presentation

What are reports for?

What are the main purposes of reports? A report can be used:

- to record routine events
- to record non-routine events
- as the basis for making decisions
- as a basis for avoiding decisions.

Reports can be purely descriptive or informative, recording routine events such as:

- monthly sales
- daily catches of fish
- weather forecast for the next four days
- national balance of payment figures.

Descriptive or informative reports can also describe non-routine events, such as accidents. They tend to be short (for example, one page), are often set out on pre-printed forms, and rarely contain sections on conclusions or recommendations. Computer reports are among the most frequently requested descriptive or informative reports. They mainly present data drawn from software databases or spreadsheets.

More analytical or persuasive reports can be used as the basis for making decisions. These reports usually present a large amount of information on topics such as the following:

- Should we seek to open up new export markets?
- Should we hire four more staff for the legal department, or should we contract the work out to independent specialists?
- Why has the northern office consistently outperformed the other three offices?
- Are we happy with our existing software, or could rival packages do a better job?

- Should we use some of our scarce resources to set up an in-house fitness facility?

- Are existing government broadcasting regulations on censorship adequate?

Analytical or persuasive reports may be short (for example, a memo or letter) or long, depending on the scope of the problem they seek to address.

Reports are vital decision-making tools, but in some situations they may be used as a basis for avoiding decisions. Researching and writing a report can take up a lot of time, and even when complete there is no guarantee that the recommendations made will be implemented. Some people who commission reports want to bring about change, while others wish to maintain the status quo while giving the impression of being open to change.

Many a report languishes unheeded, gathering dust on a shelf. This may be for good reason. Perhaps the report was no good; maybe the recommendations were impractical, or at least currently unrealistic. On the other hand, good reports are sometimes shelved because the individuals who commissioned them never had any intention of following them up (see p. 98). So if you believe in your report, and want it to have some impact, then writing it may be only the beginning. As I mentioned earlier, not only will you need to present it to your peers, but you will also have to lobby for it; you may even have to go behind the scenes to try to persuade decision-makers of the wisdom of your analysis.

Who are reports for? Know your audience

Once you have decided *what* your report is for, you need to decide *who* it is for. Who is your audience? If you need to deliver an oral report, who will you be speaking to? Is there an unofficial as well as an official audience?

Non-routine reports are normally commissioned or authorised by a person or persons further up the organisational pyramid. If the culture of your organisation encourages initiative, you may find it useful to volunteer to write and present a report, perhaps even suggesting the topic yourself.

You need to know certain things about your audience. Once you know these things, you can respond appropriately. Some questions about your audience, and your appropriate responses, are set out in table 5.3. Note that these questions and considerations may apply to audiences for routine as well as non-routine documents.

Table 5.3: analysing your audience

Factor	Question	Response
Personal style	Is the audience made up of people who prefer hearing rather than reading about something?	Put more effort into preparing the oral report than the written report
	Is the audience made up of people who prefer reading rather than hearing about something?	Put more effort into the written report than the oral report
	Is the audience made up of people who prefer detail rather than the big picture?	Concentrate on detail, but be ready to show how details fit into the big picture
	Is your audience made up of people who prefer the big picture rather than the detailed approach?	Give the big picture, but be ready to supply details to fill in the big picture
Technical background	Is your audience made up of people who are familiar and comfortable with the area's key ideas, assumptions and jargon?	Don't waste time on background explanations, as the audience may feel insulted. Jump straight in at the technical level, but be on guard against in-group complacency (which occurs when a group is cut off from reality in its world of comfortable and non-threatening assumptions)
	Is your audience made up of people who are *not* familiar and comfortable with the area's key ideas, assumptions and jargon?	Define terms, assumptions and key ideas. Make it easy for them with glossaries, simplified visual models, analogies, demonstrations and historical overviews.

Table 5.3 *(cont'd)*: analysing your audience

Factor	Question	Response
Technical background *(cont'd)*	Is your audience made up of people who are *not* familiar and comfortable with the area's key ideas, assumptions and jargon? *(cont'd)*	Don't patronise people, but put them at their ease so they feel confident enough to ask 'stupid' questions. Remember that everyone — even you — has different areas of ignorance, and that preparing a basic view of the subject may in fact give you insights that you would otherwise have missed (because you have been too close to the action to see it in perspective)
Status	Does the audience value formality?	Keep it formal
	Does the audience value informality?	Keep it informal
	Is it possible that people outside the official audience will read or hear the report?	The answer to this is always yes — or you should at least take it that it's yes, and act accordingly. It pays to be paranoid
		So, beware of sweeping generalisations, unsupported assertions, libellous statements and cheap jokes at the expense of others not present. Let your report help, not haunt, your career
Initial attitude	Positive	Good. Don't lose it by being complacent. Work on it (by paying attention to the aforementioned factors, questions and responses) to make it still more positive
	Neutral	Good. Work on it (use tips in positive attitude section) to make it more positive
	Hostile	Not so good, but not necessarily disastrous. Pay attention to the factors, questions and responses listed for positive and neutral attitudes

Factor	Question	Response
Initial attitude (cont'd)	Hostile (cont'd)	Are the audience's vested interests threatened by what you are saying? Are you in competition with them for the same scarce resources? Can you show them a mutually beneficial outcome?

Unfortunately, the answer to the questions posed in this table is usually 'All of the above', and your responses should reflect this. Remember, the difficult takes some time, and the impossible takes a little longer.

What is involved in preparing a report? A production model

All reports have some similarities in the way in which they are produced. Figure 5.2 is a model of production that shows how a report should—and should not—be produced.

Figure 5.2: the report-writing process

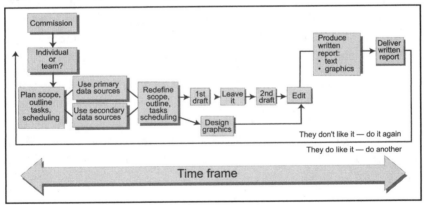

Commissioning the report

Routine reports do not require commissioning—the normal flow of work provides a structure of trigger points for report generation. Non-routine reports, however, require a specific commissioning decision. The person who commissions the report is normally part of your audience. The actual commissioning may be informal and verbal — 'Oh, Joe, can you do me a report on your monthly sales figures?' — or formal and written, set out in a letter or memo. The scope or *focus* of the report (its *terms of reference*) is defined at the time of commission.

Individual or team?

A decision needs to be made as to whether the report will be generated by an individual or a team. This will be determined by the complexity of the task and the mix of skills required. Sometimes, especially with non-routine documents, you will need to put together a writing group. On other occasions, particularly with routine documents, you will need simply to contact individuals in a loose network around you to get facts and figures.

Plan, scope, outline, tasks and scheduling

What is the report about? What is it *not* about? In non-routine documents, questions of scope will have a strong influence on the title of the report. The scope will also determine the structure of the report. At this stage, a detailed structure is not required, but an outline is. The outline should set out the sections, headings, points and subpoints of the overall document. Your report's outline will bear more than a passing resemblance to the final document's table of contents.

The scope and outline will help to determine the tasks of research and production, and the time frame or schedule within which these tasks need to be achieved. At this stage the types of questions that need to be asked include: how long do I have to complete the report? What resources do I have? What specific tasks can the report be broken down into?

Primary and secondary sources of data

Once decisions about scope, structure, tasks and scheduling have been made, primary data can be collected and analysed, and secondary data can be studied. Sources of primary data include questionnaires, interviews, experiments, observations and company records. Primary data does not exist until it is created by researchers or people who collect data as part of their jobs. Once such data exists, it can form the basis of secondary data, which is published in various forms, including books, journals, statistical bulletins and electronic databases.

Report writers must determine whether there is a need for primary data, secondary data or both. Secondary data is easier and cheaper to collect than primary data, but it may be too general or out of date. Much will depend on the situation, the problem to be studied, the nature of existing data, and the availability of resources to create new data and retrieve existing data. Nevertheless, it makes sense to check secondary data first — if this information is good enough, there will be no need to go to the trouble of creating primary data.

Redefine the scope, outline, tasks and scheduling

Once primary and secondary data have been collected and studied, it may be that the scope or focus of the report needs to be adjusted. At this stage you may discover that:

- what you thought was going to be a general study will simply be too big, and you now need to narrow the focus

- what you thought was a small-scale phenomenon has much wider ramifications, and a broader approach is needed

- the data provides answers but also raises new questions

- promising areas turn out to be dead ends

- initially unpromising areas turn out to be goldmines

- some data proves to be unavailable

- some data proves to be so rich that it is difficult to manage

- some areas are interesting, but the time to explore them is not available

- your enthusiasm for some areas declines

- your enthusiasm for other areas increases.

A redefinition of scope is a fairly normal occurrence and nothing to worry about. Of course, it may also entail a redefinition of the report's outline structure, and of the appropriate tasks and scheduling.

Design graphics

Once the outline is clear, decisions can be made about what type of graphic communication needs to be included in the document. If there is a chance that you will have to present your report, keep in mind that graphics prepared for the page may not necessarily work as projected graphics in a presentation.

Draft, set aside, redraft

Now the drafting begins. Remember that what you write now will not necessarily be what your audience eventually reads or hears. Very few of us can write so flawlessly that our first draft can be used as the final draft. Expect to complete at least two drafts (more if the need arises). If time permits, and you should try to schedule the work so that it does, set the draft document aside before rereading it and attempting the next draft. You can get too close to a piece of work and lose perspective.

All your ideas and insights will not simply appear, fully formed, in your first draft. Once your mind is set loose on a problem, it will produce all kinds of straightforward and quirky perspectives over time. It's not uncommon to have a blinding insight into a problem analysed in a report well after a document has been finished. Preparing reports is rarely associated with creativity, but the analysis involved in preparing reports is part of the wider problem-solving process, and that process is often a creative one. Work with the creative impulse by allowing time to pass while you turn your attention to other matters, returning to start the second draft with a refreshed mind and, with luck, new perspectives.

Edit, produce, deliver

Once you have completed your final draft, you can edit it more closely. Editing entails checking the logical flow of information, the clarity of expression, the language mechanics, the layout, the conventions of citation, and so forth. If you are required to prepare an oral as well as a written report, this is an opportune time to edit or repackage the content of the written report so that it is more suitable for spoken delivery.

The production of the document is no minor task. Aesthetic decisions about layout design and overall look have to be made and then executed professionally. As mentioned earlier, the report's visual appeal can substantially influence its acceptance. Make sure that any graphic illustrations enhance your message, rather than detract from it.

Delivery of a written report may be a straightforward process, without much formal procedure. Presenting an oral report tends to involve more conventions.

Evaluate

Do they like it? Do they hate it? Either outcome may point to further report writing in the future. If your audience responds negatively, you may be asked to go back and do it again. If the audience likes it, you may be asked to do others. It won't do your career any harm to be known as someone who can be relied on to produce a useful report.

Analytical reports

Now for 'the big one'—the analytical or research report. Most formal analytical or investigative reports have a standard structure, although some individual writers and organisations have developed their own variations. This type of report has three main sections, with items in each section being either essential or optional. Table 5.4 lists what may be involved in this large document.

Table 5.4: structure of an analytical report

Section	Essential	Optional
Front matter	Title page	Cover
	Summary/synopsis	Terms of reference
	Table of contents	Memo/letter of transmittal
		List of figures
		List of tables

Table 5.4 *(cont'd)*: structure of an analytical report

Section	Essential	Optional
Body	Introduction	Figures (diagrams)
	Discussion	Tables (data arrays)
	Conclusions	Plates (photographs)
	Recommendations	
Endmatter	References/bibliography	Index
		Glossary
		Appendices

Good news and bad news — structure and the politics of persuasion

A report can have either a direct structure (in which you state the gist of your message at the start) or an indirect structure (in which you defer this statement). Which structure you choose will often depend on the reception you expect from your audience — if you expect them to be happy to receive your message, this is a 'good news' situation and a direct approach should be used. If you think your audience will be unhappy to receive your message, or may have reservations about it, then this is a 'bad news' situation and the indirect approach is preferred (compare good news and bad news letters, p. 20).

The indirect approach may be used when you are describing a complex situation, with a number of challenging but nevertheless soluble problems, and you simply need to introduce your audience to such solutions before they react prematurely to the potentially negative aspects of the message. Writing in this form will stretch your abilities as a writer, but it's a challenge worth overcoming.

When deciding whether to use a direct or indirect structure (see table 5.5), you need to consider the sequence in which you will present your argument, paying particular attention to your summary or synopsis. Choose your words carefully according to what you are trying to achieve — when using the indirect structure, you are not aiming to be dishonest, but rather trying to create a context that will stimulate considered rather than impulsive and reactive decision making.

Table 5.5: direct and indirect report structures

Direct structure: summary section wording	Indirect structure: summary section wording
This report examines the need for policy measures to cope with new budget constraints, particularly in the area of salaries.	This report examines the need for policy measures to cope with new budget constraints, particularly in the area of salaries.
It is recommended that: • band A staff take a pay cut of 12 per cent • band B staff take a pay cut of 6.5 per cent, with all overtime eliminated • no expenses be allowable unless given prior approval by DOF.	Various issues are examined, including the possibility of: • pay cuts • reducing or eliminating overtime • changing approval mechanisms for expenses.

Cover

The document may be secured in a folder or even professionally bound as a book. The line between professional and non-professional document production has been blurred in the past few years with the increased availability and sophistication of computer word processing packages. Now, all but the briefest reports are likely to have a cover. It is not difficult for a report writer today to design and create a cover featuring stylish typography and images. People do judge books by their covers, and it is important that the cover of a report is inviting enough to motivate the prospective reader to look further.

A folder or binding will protect the report and give the document a stronger identity, making it less likely to be lost in the paperwork that builds up on many people's desks. Durability and visibility may help ensure that the report is placed on a shelf, where it can be easily retrieved, rather than filed away where it may sink without trace. An attractive cover will help; if possible, ensure that the report title is on the front and on the spine.

As with all organisational communications, the house style and organisational culture are paramount. If your cover is likely to be regarded by the organisation commissioning the report as being too radical, distracting or wasteful, then follow the accepted conventions.

Letter/memorandum of transmittal

You may be required to compose a letter or memorandum of transmittal for a report (see table 5.6). This is the most personal part of the communication exercise and the most direct message from writer to reader.

Table 5.6: typical wording used in a letter or memo of transmission

Letter/memo of transmittal section	Typical wording
Salutation to the person who commissioned or authorised the report	*Dear Mr/Ms Smith ...*
Statement of purpose of letter/memo	*Here is the report on ... you requested ...*
Brief overview or summary of report	*In this report you will find ...*
Acknowledgements to people who helped you with your investigations	*Several people proved to be of great assistance to me ...*
Courteous close	*Thank you for the opportunity to investigate ... If you have any questions about the report, please contact me ...*

Some writers will include a brief mention of their recommendations in the letter or memo. Whether you decide to do so will depend on factors such as whether your recommendations are controversial and you would prefer the reader to read the rationale behind them before being confronted with them, as well as on space constraints.

If the report is transmitted internally, then a memo of transmittal, in standard memo format, is used. If a report is transmitted to someone in another organisation, then a letter of transmittal, in standard letter format, is used.

Title

The title of the report should clearly describe to the reader what the report is about. Remember, what is obvious to you in a title may not be obvious to your reader—you may be too close to the issue, taking for granted a knowledge of certain concepts or jargon that may not be familiar to your reader. Try out a number of titles on people who are more removed from the problem to get an idea of which title works best.

If the report has a cover, the wording on the cover and the title page should be identical. Your title is a promise to the reader and the report itself should fulfil that promise. The promise will not be realised, for example, if the scope of the report, as represented by your original title, has since shifted. It is perfectly normal for the scope of a report to shift several times in the course of the document's preparation; for instance, when new information leads to different perspectives or conclusions. One of the most often overlooked tasks in editing a report is ensuring that the title actually sums up the content of the final document. Make sure you promise what you deliver and deliver what you promise.

Contents page

The contents page lists each element in the front matter, the body of the report and the endmatter—with the exception of the letter or memo of transmittal (which should be attached to the front of the report), the cover, the title page and the table of contents itself. All sections and subsections of the report are listed, along with their respective page numbers. The table of contents, which will probably be similar to the outline you developed in the report planning process, is the reader's roadmap. The bigger and more complex the report, the more important a table of contents becomes.

List of illustrations

A list of illustrations may be helpful for larger reports with a substantial number of graphics. For more complex documents it may also be useful to provide separate lists for figures and tables. Note that photographs are sometimes referred to as 'plates'.

Summary/synopsis/abstract

Summary, synopsis and abstract are three terms sometimes used interchangeably in report writing. *Synopsis* and *abstract* tend to be used in more academic and scientific documents, while *summary* is the less academic, more general usage. The term *executive summary* is also common in non-academic publications. In this brief section you need to summarise the entire content of the body of the report, including the introduction, the main discussion, and your conclusions and recommendations. Keep in mind the considerations of the direct versus indirect approach.

At the risk of a bruised ego, you should recognise that the summary is as far as many of your readers will get in your report, or indeed will want to get. They want the quick version, so you must ensure your summary is good.

This report, by its very length, defends itself against the risk of being read.
Winston Churchill

Introduction

The introduction should inform the reader about some or all of the following:

- *Background.* Why was the report commissioned? What circumstances led people to believe that a report was needed?

- *Purpose.* What is the purpose of the report?

- *Scope.* What issues are discussed in the report? What issues are not covered? (This is also known as the *brief* or *terms of reference*.)

- *Research methods.* How was the data in this report obtained? What types of primary and/or secondary data were used? Does the data limit the report in any way?

- *Definition of terms.* What specific terminology is used that the lay reader may not be familiar with? (If there are more than five or six such terms, you should consider including a separate glossary of terms in the endmatter of the report.)

- *Limitations.* What constraints (for example, time, resources, data) were there on the exercise?

- *Assumptions.* What has the writer assumed about background, concepts, language and reader awareness?

Discussion

The main discussion or findings section is the real meat of the report. It will almost certainly be the largest section, and its preparation will entail the most work. Ensure that your argument is clearly developed, and is broken up logically into sections and subsections, with appropriate headings and subheadings.

There are numerous ways in which to develop an argument (see table 5.7). It is possible to combine some of these methods and given that they all have their limitations, this is sometimes desirable. However, be sure you do not confuse your reader (and possibly yourself).

Table 5.7: some argument development methods

Argument development method	Approach
Chronological	From then to now, and on into the future
Inductive	From the particular to the general
Deductive	From the general to the particular
Geographical	From one area/section/state/country/planet to another
Topical	From one subject to another
Problem/solution	The problem is … The solution/options are …
Pros/cons	The advantages are … The disadvantages are …
5W/H	Explanation of what, where, when, why, who, how
Ideal/reality	What we would like is … What we are stuck with is …

After outlining the problem, it is quite valid to discuss a range of options or alternative responses (the problem–solution approach to developing an argument lends itself particularly to this method). These alternatives can then be referred to when making recommendations. Remember to confine yourself to facts in the discussion section of your report. If you have opinions, you should reserve them for the conclusions and recommendations sections.

Conclusions

The conclusions section provides an overview of the report's content. Here you can provide your own interpretation of the information that has been set out, answering the question 'What does all this mean?' You can also provide a specific context for the recommendations you are about to make. Typical conclusions may take the following form:

> It is clear that the photocopying centre cannot cope with certain peak workloads, particularly when we are conducting audits of large clients...

> Options 2 and 6 are attractive if solely financial criteria are applied, but would be unpopular with staff in the eastern zone plant. Options 1, 3, 4 and 5 would be less unpopular, but clearly would entail greater expense, particularly if we buy rather than lease...

Recommendations

In the final section of the report, the recommendations, you propose specific actions that should flow from the conclusions. Keep in mind that just as recommendations are based on conclusions, so conclusions are based on the information discussed in the body of the report.

You should not introduce new material in the conclusions or recommendations sections. It is common for report writers to reach conclusions and recommendations whose foundation has not been demonstrated in the body of the document. It's only natural—your mind, turning over the problem, delivers up novel solutions that may be unconnected to the facts as you have presented them. Don't maroon your good ideas, however; rather, grasp the perhaps unpleasant fact that you may now need to go back and revise the body, creating a foundation for your new conclusions and recommendations.

If the introduction, discussion and conclusions are part of the problem-solving process, then the recommendations are part of the decision-making process. Because of this, some commissioners of reports exclude recommendations from the scope, brief or terms of reference of the report, believing that they can produce their own action plans based on what they have read.

It may be useful to number your recommendations. This will make discussion of them easier. You may also choose to place recommendations in priority order.

Some writers prefer to give recommendations in the body of the report, at the end of each section. This style is adopted particularly with large reports. It can be a useful way of linking a response directly to the problem discussed. If you choose to do this, it is still helpful to list all of the recommendations together, and the best place for such a list is where most readers would expect to find it — at the end of the report, following the conclusions.

Typical recommendations may take the following forms:

> It is recommended that all systems continue operating the Microsoft XP operating system for the next six months. At that time, Data Processing will report on options to convert systems to the Linux–JT operating system.

> 3. Option 3 (subcontract new accounts to external consultants via competitive tendering) should be trialled for 12 months.

References, bibliography and endnotes

With your conclusions and recommendations, you have completed the main parts of the report. All that remains is the endmatter. Here the reference list usually comes first. This section lists all the materials you have referred to in your research and used in the report.

Appendices or attachments

You may wish to include material with your report that does not belong in it (perhaps it is too large, or would be of interest to only part of your audience) but still may be useful for the reader to refer to. Such material is included at the back of the report as an appendix.

If you have more than one set of such material, then each should be separately identified (for example, Appendix A, B, C or Appendix I, II, III ...). This material may include raw data, copies of questionnaires used, interview transcripts, maps, copies of legislation appropriate to the topic, detailed historical background, complex graphics, computer software demonstrating what you are talking about, a videotape — in short, anything that does not fit tidily into the structure of the written report.

My most important piece of advice is to tell all you would-be writers: when you write, try to leave out all the parts the readers skip.
Elmore Leonard

Glossary, list of abbreviations and index

If your report is particularly complex, involving terminology that may be unfamiliar to some of your audience, consider creating a glossary in which you list and define these terms. Similarly, create a list of, or key to, possibly confusing abbreviations (acronyms, initialisms or shortened words). If your glossary or list of abbreviations extends beyond about ten entries, perhaps you should consider whether you are in danger of losing your audience.

If your report is extensive (say, over twenty pages), consider creating an index. Indexing can be time-consuming, but word processing software has taken much of the labour out of it. An index will provide your audience with a more detailed 'navigation map' than is possible with the table of contents.

Table 5.8 is a checklist for ensuring that your analytical or research report has the minimum number of weaknesses and the maximum number of strengths.

Table 5.8: an editing checklist for analytical reports

Feature	Detail	✓
Cover (where separate from title page)	Durability	
	Attractiveness	
	Identification (title)	
Letter/memo of transmittal	Salutation	
	Statement of letter's purpose	

Feature	Detail	✓
Letter/memo of transmittal (cont'd)	Brief overview of report	
	Acknowledgements	
	Courteous close	
Title	Accurate description of scope/contents	
	Same as on cover	
Contents page	Accurate reflection of structure	
	Accurate reflection of pagination	
List of illustrations (optional)	Accurate reflection of sequence	
Synopsis/summary/ abstract	Accurate summary of body, endmatter	
Introduction	Background given	
	Purpose described	
	Scope defined	
	Research methods described	
	Terms defined	
Discussion	Argument developed logically	
	Factual approach — no opinions yet	
	Balanced approach — not biased in what is presented or omitted	
Conclusions	Based on matter discussed	
Recommendations	Based on matter discussed and conclusions	
References, bibliography and endnotes	Complete	
	Consistent use of citation system	
Appendices/attachments	Complete	
Glossary (optional)	Complete	
Index (optional)	Complete	

Table 5.8 *(cont'd)*: an editing checklist for analytical reports

Feature	Detail	✓
Structure	Clear and consistent	
	Headings accurate	
	Hierarchical structure reflects correct exposition of argument	
	Headings grammatically parallel	
Layout/document design	Adequate white space	
	Fonts—minimal variation	
	Fonts—consistent use	
	Graphics placed appropriately	
Graphics	Appropriate	
	Identified	
	Referred to in text	
Pagination	Accurate	
Referencing	Correct	
	Consistent	
Quotation	Correct	
	Consistent	
	Legitimate—no plagiarism or distortion	
Language	Clear, readable style	
	Style consistent between sections	
	Grammar correct	
	Spelling correct	
	Punctuation correct	
	No unnecessary jargon	
	No clichés	
	No redundancies	

Feature	Detail	✓
Language (cont'd)	More concrete than abstract	
	No repetition	
	Paragraphing clear	

Avoid games report writers (and commissioners) play

Those who write bad reports tend to fall into certain traps; some writers even play mind games with their audiences. Here are some of the games played by report writers (and commissioners) and some pitfalls that less-experienced writers fall for. Avoid all of them like the plague.

Preconceived bias

Make sure that you take a balanced approach in your discussion, covering all points of view and options, or at least as many as possible.

A common mistake committed by report writers is to come to a topic with preconceived views, and then create a biased document in support of those opinions. Not only is this unprofessional, it's also unwise. There will always be someone in your audience who can, and will, challenge your approach, which may damage your reputation. It also means that any good material in your document can more easily be dismissed. Get in first before they do, and pre-emptively rebut ideas, products and processes that you don't like.

Perhaps the worst outcome for biased documents is when no-one in the audience picks up the shortcomings in time, and action is taken on the basis of the document — with sometimes catastrophic results.

Acquired bias

Another related pitfall is that of acquired bias, which occurs when topic loyalty or capture sets in. A report involves much work, and there is a tendency for some writers to invest so much time, energy and resources into the document that they become intellectually and emotionally committed to the ideas they are presenting. In some cases writers may even turn a blind eye to the ideas' weaknesses and may find it impossible to finally recommend against what they are writing about. These writers have become captured by the topic. You should always be ready to write negative recommendations—to give, for example, a no-go rather than a go recommendation to a project—in the spirit of even-handedness. If not, rest assured that your worst enemies will point out your blind spots.

Job creationism

Topic loyalty or capture also occurs when writers begin to sense that their recommendations could enhance their own career paths—'this is a good idea, and by the way, I'm available to put it into practice'. This is human nature, but be careful of falling into such a trap—or at least do it with such style and rationale that no-one is aware that you are doing it.

Timidity

Timidity occurs when report writers decide to present as unchallenging a document as possible, even when the evidence suggests that faults need to be pointed out and radical changes may need to be recommended. Timidity often occurs in organisations with a 'shoot the messenger' culture and where 'groupthink' is prevalent. In such organisations, unfortunately, it may make sense to deliver a 'don't make waves' document—but only in the short term, as the consequences of inaction usually make themselves felt eventually.

Whitewash

A whitewash occurs when a report writer conceals the true (and unpleasant) nature of the problem the report was meant to investigate. In these situations the guilty, or problem-creators, escape judgement.

Vendetta

The opposite of a whitewash is a vendetta, or witch hunt, which occurs when a report writer aggressively ascribes responsibility or guilt for a problem, and sometimes to those who do not deserve it. Some folk wisdom can be found on the internet about the phases of a project:

1   exultation

2   disenchantment

3   search for the guilty

4   punishment of the innocent

5   praise for the uninvolved.

A vendetta report does all of these things. Note that a report can be both a whitewash and a vendetta.

Boosterism

Boosterism simply means writing propaganda and public relations rather than analysis. For example, a report writer may simply sing the praises of the organisation's products without realistically assessing rival products and the wider market. These are SO-SO documents—they avoid SWOT (strengths, weakenesses, opportunities and threats) and only concentrate on strengths and opportunities. Boosterism usually leads to the same disastrous results as timidity.

Flag-waving

While boosterism refers to the broader scale of just what it is that an organisation does, flag-waving narrows the focus. A flag-waving report is a self-serving one that over-emphasises the virtues and importance of one section of the organisation—the report writer's section.

Hobby horses

Hobby horses are pet projects or ideas of report writers that are given undue prominence in a report.

Sloppiness

Sloppy reports are notable for poor research, over-dependence on low-quality sources such as internet sites and sales literature, and often show signs of plagiarism and cut-and-paste of pre-existing documents.

Reactivity

Reactive report writers are always fighting the last war, producing post-mortems on situations but offering very little in the way of future orientation, proactive planning or fresh thought.

Decision avoidance

As I've already mentioned, reports are sometimes commissioned in order to avoid decisions as much as to aid decisions. Less than ethical report commissioners may hope that a problem will go away or be buried by asking someone to engage in time-wasting report research and writing. The hidden agenda of the commissioner can be carried out by writing terms of reference that are too narrow, ignoring the report, or simply rejecting its findings.

Learning how to write powerful, winning proposals can be one of the most important business skills you ever acquire. This skill enables you to communicate your solutions effectively and persuasively to your clients and your colleagues. In doing so, you'll be meeting their needs for information and insight while achieving your own goals. Besides, writing a proposal is often the most truly professional thing you do.

Tom Sant

Proposals, tenders and submissions

A document quite similar to the report is the proposal or submission. People write proposals, tenders or submissions to obtain funding or resources to achieve certain goals. The goals may involve, for example:

- winning a contract from a company to deliver goods and/or services
- obtaining government funding to set up and manage a program or enterprise.

Proposal is generally the preferred term in North American business and government circles, while *submission* tends to be used in British and Commonwealth business and government circles. Bid documents for public sector program and private sector philanthropic funding tend to be called *grant applications* in North America.

Government departments and agencies disbursing funds call for submissions or for business plans. Within the British/Commonwealth culture, the term *tender* is sometimes applied to a document used to bid for a contract to provide goods and/or services. A *submission* can also be a document containing information and opinion that is submitted or given to a government committee of inquiry into a particular issue (with the committee usually producing a report, based in part on submissions from various concerned parties).

Because proposals, tenders and submissions usually require more in the way of documentation to demonstrate credibility (for example, documentation about staffing, costings and project timelines), writers often use not only word-processing software but also project-management software to create the final body of documentation.

Submissions or proposals often have a similar structure to reports, but there are some notable differences as shown in table 5.9 (overleaf).

Most of these differences and similarities are self-evident, but special mention should be made of the lobbying process. Decision-makers can be influenced by the documents presented to them, but lobbying or active persuasion can also influence them after the document has been presented. Such lobbying may take the following forms:

- making continual phone calls to an administrator who is considering a number of submissions

- arranging an 'accidental' social encounter with a manager who helps choose proposals for an organisation

- talking to politicians who may influence a submission/ proposal process

- providing free transport, accommodation, hospitality and an inspection tour for influential decision-makers.

Table 5.9: reports versus proposals/tenders/submissions

	Reports	Proposals/tenders/ submissions
Role of writer?	Apparently neutral; makes disinterested choice among possible solutions	Interested party; pursues advocacy of one solution
Is present writer same as future implementer?	Not necessarily	Usually
Pattern?	Recommendations mentioned briefly at beginning, then in detail at conclusion	Entire document can be a recommendation
Nature of persuasion?	Implicit, low profile	Explicit, high profile
Message?	... needs to be done about ...	Let us do ... about ...
Focus?	Phenomenon, problem	Project, solution
Are action plan, budget, schedule, staffing details, details of writers included?	Not necessarily	Yes
How many per situation?	Usually only one	Often more than one
Software used in preparation	Word processing, perhaps presentation	Word processing, perhaps presentation and project management
Relationship between writer and reader?	Patron/artist; research commissioner/researcher	Buyer/seller
Action stance?	Usually reactive	Proactive and reactive
Comes from?	Usually from inside the organisation	Inside and outside the organisation
Organisational culture?	More routine; less competition-driven	Less routine; more competition-driven
Formalised structure?	Medium	High, medium, low
Lobbying likely after delivery of document?	Less likely	More likely

Writers of proposals, tenders and submissions tend to be more involved with lobbying than writers of reports, but it would be wrong to think that report writers are not at all involved in lobbying. All organisations—indeed all human communication—is political to some extent.

Some recommendations on preparation of these documents are set out in table 5.10.

Table 5.10: tenders/proposals/submissions—do's and don'ts

Do's	Don'ts
Always address the question asked; do not include irrelevant material to pad out the answer	Never rely on a last-minute courier delivery; give yourself as much time as possible to deliver the document
Follow the protocol of the document	Do not work as individuals when preparing the response
Ensure you can deliver what you say in the document	Do not be complacent about your relationship with the client; you need to focus on the future
Use a compliance table to demonstrate your ability to meet the client's requirements	Do not think as yourself or your business when preparing: always have the client's perspective in mind
Have an independent person review the document; a fresh pair of eyes may identify things you have missed because of your narrow focus	Never underestimate the competition
Read the client's document thoroughly to ensure you understand what they need	Do not include irrelevant content or extensive marketing material
Always check that the client information is correct	Do not assume the client is ignorant—they may know more than they indicate in the tender specification
Always keep the client's specific requirements in mind—you must demonstrate your understanding of what the client requires	Do not treat questions in isolation—they are part of a larger response
Always ask questions to make sure you understand	Don't be afraid to ask questions—the more information you have, the better prepared you are

Table 5.10 *(cont'd)*: tenders/proposals/submissions — do's and don'ts

Do's	Don'ts
Always ask for a debriefing after the decision is known, regardless of whether you win or lose; identify what worked and what did not work for development of future responses	Never deliver a document that has not been reviewed and/or edited
Provide contact details including name, phone number, email and office address	

Source: Adapted from TenderSearch, © 2004 TenderSearch <www.tendersearch.com.au>.

Try it yourself

1   One of the problems first-time report writers have is implementing headings and sub-headings — that is, imposing a visual and hierarchical form on their words. Copy at least one document into your word processor, and then use the outline view function in your word processor to impose a multi-level structure.

2   Another problem experienced by first-time report writers is distinguishing between conclusions and recommendations. Conclusions sum up the situation, while recommendations are action steps flowing from that overview. Find a document with only conclusions; for example, an essay from your secondary or post-secondary education days, then write recommendations based upon the conclusions you reached in that earlier document. It doesn't matter if the recommendations are far-fetched (for example, Hamlet should now do this ...).

3   Think of an issue or situation in your current workplace. Imagine that you have just written a report on it. Now, following the models on p. 85, write a direct structure summary and an indirect structure summary.

4   Find out if any report documents exist in a workplace you are currently in. Dig them out, and review them in light of what you have

---

learnt in this chapter. Compare them with the sample report in the Appendix (p. 133), and the fault list on p. 157.

5   Explore your word processor, and find out what report templates are on it, or available online. Review at least two of them, and see what use you could make of them.

Chapter 6

Online writing— emails and websites

Newer online or electronic forms of communication—email and text for websites—involve mastering some new techniques; however, none of the skills associated with writing paper documents will be wasted here—on the contrary. The more you learn about writing by drafting and editing letters, memos and reports, the more likely it is that you will be a more effective writer of emails and web text.

The offline world goes online

The online world began in 1969, when the Advanced Research Project Agency (ARPA) of the US Department of Defense developed ARPANET, a computer network that facilitated communication between researchers at dispersed locations. It was also designed to provide a communication system decentralised and robust enough to take over should a nuclear attack disrupt conventional, centralised systems.

Email addresses using the @ symbol were used for the first time in 1972. The World Wide Web, which constitutes a large part of the internet as we know it today, was developed in 1989 at CERN (Conseil Européen pour la Recherche Nucléaire, or the European Organisation for Particle Physics Research) in Switzerland. Since 1969 the growth in online communication has been phenomenal.

Because of this rapid growth, the internet and the modes of communication it has made possible are still very much evolving, and the web environment is simultaneously both highly structured and anarchic.

The internet, which is in fact a network of networks, facilitates a number of forms of electronic communication, including:

- electronic mail (or email)
- the World Wide Web
- newsgroups, or online discussion/chat groups
- file transfer protocol (FTP) (links to data files)
- instant messaging (IM) (real-time chat between identified individuals).

Two offshoots of the internet are intranets and extranets. An intranet is a computer network that serves the internal needs of an organisation, creating a virtual space that allows local email exchange and use of web pages not available to the general public. An extranet is a network, external to an organisation, that links two or more intranets and creates a virtual space for communication between them. Extranets support B2B (business-to-business) communication, facilitating the secure interchange of information between organisations such as procurement/ordering details, maintenance requests and inventory checks.

People and organisations access various electronic communication channels via different types of hardware. In medium to large organisations powerful mainframe computers act as servers, providing resources to the desktop or portable computers of individual staff members. Network access is obtained through telephone lines, cable or satellite connections. An essential linking technology is the modem, which enables a computer to transmit and receive information over a standard telephone line. The channel or medium of transmission (whether phone line, high-capacity cable or satellite) defines the bandwidth of the signal that can be carried. Fibre-optic cable, satellite and ISDN (integrated services digital network) are broadband channels, which can carry multiple messages simultaneously; conventional telephone lines, which have much lower capacity, can carry only one message at a time.

The lower the capacity of your modem and transmission channel, the slower and less capable your internet connection will be. Such constraints have implications for the size of emails and attachments that can be sent, and for the loading times of web pages (the more complex the page, the slower the loading). Web pages are viewed through enabling computer programs called browsers, and can be located via search engines.

Writing on the net

In this chapter I will examine writing approaches to two forms of online communication—email and websites.

Emails, which are generally informal, unstructured and unformatted plain text, are perhaps closer to the memo genre than to the letter. They are a quick and cheap means of exchanging messages, virtues that have begun to cause problems, with junk or spam email increasing exponentially in recent years.

As a communication form, websites may be usefully compared to advertising brochures, magazines and journals. Web documents, however, vary wildly in quality, with the substantial and enduring existing alongside the trivial and ephemeral. Content is, for the most part, unregulated, so that problematic material (pornography, hate sites) exists side by side with more mainstream coverage.

There is much contention about what this all means. Some web enthusiasts see spam, porn and junk information as signs of a vibrant entrepreneurial culture that will help develop e-commerce (electronic commerce) and hasten the day when the whole planet communicates online. Others are more pessimistic, seeing these developments as counterproductive and likely to strangle online communication before it goes much further.

Online writing—mosaic and 3-D

Traditional writing in paper texts is by definition linear and narrative—that is, writers most often start at the beginning and proceed to the end. This is the case with most works of fiction, in which creative writing is an end in itself. The linear approach is also fairly standard in documents such as essays, letters, memos and reports (see chapters 1 to 5), although they may include endmatter or attachments (appendices, bibliographies) that go beyond the nominal end of the document and that readers may choose to look at or not. (Report readers may get no further than the summary.)

In other areas of non-fiction publication, the words are more likely to be a means to an end, the end usually being to obtain specific information. We may choose to skim and scan workplace documents, reading relevant material rather than every deathless word (except in certain circumstances, where legality or safety is concerned).

In the case of textbooks, readers may use the table of contents, index or other navigation tools to locate the information they need, while ignoring the rest. With a phone book, directory, catalogue or other reference book, they will also consult only that information they need, disregarding the rest. Most people read instruction manuals in order to *do* rather than to *learn* and so may pick only the content most immediately relevant (a strategy not without peril, of course). In all such texts, although we may not always read them from beginning to end, but rather select the information we need, the documents are in most cases constructed in a linear way.

Online writing, on the other hand, while it developed from traditional writing, tends more to non-linear or mosaic forms than traditional print-based narrative and descriptive text. Conventional writing is two-dimensional—a page has horizontal and vertical dimensions. In most language traditions, the reader starts at the top left of the page, moves across the line to the right margin, then repeats the process, moving down the page, turning the page when necessary. Online writing adds a third 'dimension' within the screen space with hypertext, or electronic links to other parts of the document or to other documents or websites (see figure 6.1).

Figure 6.1: the 3-D mosaic of writing in the online space

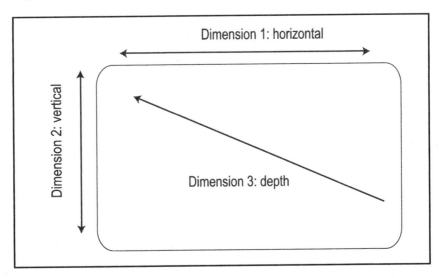

Therefore, a book on animals may be constructed as shown in figure 6.2.

Figure 6.2: a linear/narrative approach

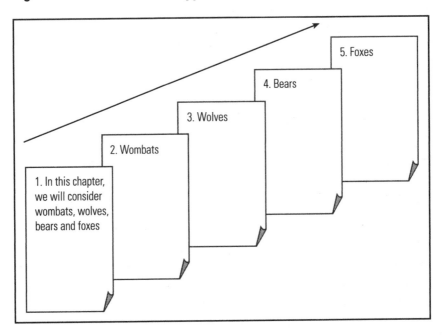

On the other hand, a website on the same topic may be constructed as shown in figure 6.3.

Figure 6.3: a non-linear/mosaic approach — hyperlinking is two-way

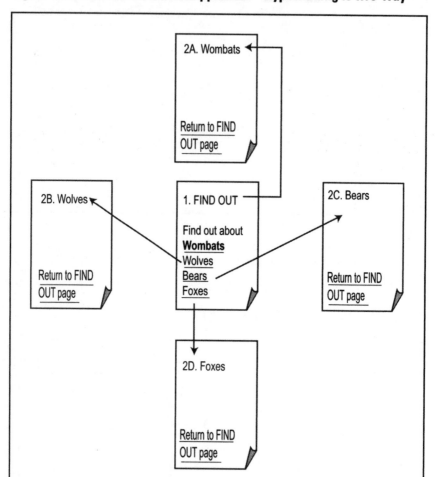

In the non-linear approach, hypertext links are indicated by underlined text, often in a different colour to indicate that the words are 'hot' — that is, electronically linked to other pages or sites.

In the non-linear example (figure 6.3), the reader can access online information (here the second-level pages are labelled 2A, 2B, 2C and 2D) in any sequence, rather than being constrained by the linear approach most often followed by a book treatment of the same content.

The reader may choose to 'drill down' through multiple structural levels of information or follow a different sequence entirely. This type of branching structure is common in online games and learning modules. The process has much in common with flow-charting, where 'if-then' logic is used to cover a variety of permutations and combinations of events. The online screen, then, has advantages and disadvantages when communicating information (see table 6.1).

Table 6.1: advantages and disadvantages of online/mosaic writing when compared with linear/narrative exposition in hard copy

Advantages	Disadvantages
Able to hyperlink areas of content	Less information can be contained in a typical single screen than in a typical printed page
Gives the reader more control when interacting with the content and determining the sequence in which the content will be explored or navigated	Screen text may not be as legible as printed page
Able to show movement or animation	More reader effort is needed to scroll horizontally and vertically through screen text than to look at different parts of a printed page
Able to convey sound	Readers navigating via hot links can miss material when they choose their own pathway through content
	Lack of tactility
	Possible time lags, especially when low-powered modems or slow computers are used

Implications for online writing when compared with conventional writing include the following:

- Writers may have to use fewer words on a screen than on a page.

- Writers have to reconceptualise the screen page, where the text may be closer to a printed paragraph than a printed page.

- Writers may have to break up content into information blocks connected by hypertext links.

- Writers may need to arrange their content according to priority after considering behavioural factors (impatience, fatigue) and technological factors (computer functionality, mouse type).

  ¤ Priority 1: 3rd dimension (use hypertext)

  ¤ Priority 2: 2nd dimension (allow vertical scrolling)

  ¤ Priority 3: 1st dimension (allow horizontal scrolling).

Page size needs to be set so as to minimise the reader's need to scroll horizontally or vertically. Rather than creating a page that is too big for the screen, seek other solutions; one may lie in the third dimension, with hot links.

Email

Email, electronic text messages sent over a communications network between computers, has become the principal means of communicating in many organisations and among many individuals. I'm now going to discuss different aspects of email, including the style or register of language used, design and layout factors, the use of attachments, some general writing and document management guidelines, and warnings about some of the hazards of the genre.

Email style

The writing style used in email tends to be more informal than that used in letters and even memos. For example, email frequently dispenses with formal salutations ('Dear …') and closes (for example, 'Yours sincerely'), while contractions ('I'm', 'it's'), abbreviations, colloquialisms, slang and jargon are common.

Naomi Baron, a specialist in language analysis, concludes that email:

- is in some ways like speech (use of first- and second-person pronouns, present tense, unedited)

- is helping to develop a level conversational playing field (hierarchical distinctions within organisations, preserved by the mechanics of formal written communication, begin to break down, with people at junior levels communicating directly but informally with people at senior levels)

- encourages personal disclosure (sometimes email writers will reveal opinions and information online that they would not in face-to-face conversation or in a more formal document)

- can become emotional (some email writers indulge in 'flaming' —strongly worded expressions (for example, of outrage or abuse) that they would not necessarily use in face-to-face conversation).

One reason why email style often reflects the informality of conversation is that users recognise the impermanence of the form. Other significant factors include:

- Emails are commonly unformatted plain text (without varying fonts, type treatment, colour and design features). Even when complex formatting of messages is attempted, there is no guarantee that with current technology your reader will receive your message in the form you sent it.

- Spell-checking and grammar/style checking features of email software generally lag behind those of word processing programs (although post-2002 versions are not bad).

Some of these tendencies may change over time. Ten years ago faxes tended to be more informal in style, but as they became an accepted part of professional communication, their style became more formal. Email is following that path now, with chat rooms and instant messaging filling the more informal communication roles. The formality–informality continuum in communication style today is suggested in this continuum diagram (figure 6.4).

Figure 6.4: a formality–informality continuum of communication modes

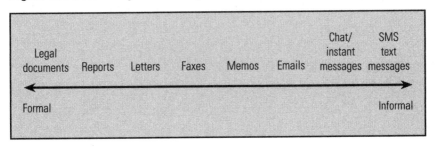

As in any form of communication, to a certain extent appropriate style depends on the receiver or reader. Generally speaking, you should use a more formal style when:

- the receiver holds a more senior position in the organisational hierarchy than you

- the receiver is outside your organisation

- the receiver is unlikely to be familiar with jargon or terminology used in your industry, organisation or area

- there is a chance that your correspondence will be referred to by others, will be archived or will form a part of important transactions (and all of these considerations are becoming more, not less, likely).

There is no quicker way for two executives to get out of touch with each other than to retire to the seclusion of their offices and write each other notes.
R Alec Mackenzie, *The Time Trap*

Writing email—what structure?

The structuring or sequencing of information critically influences the effectiveness of these communications. In chapter 1, I discussed direct versus indirect methods of structuring messages (see p. 21 and p. 28). In email, direct structuring, getting your message up front, is usually the most suitable approach. Consider using the the MADE formula for structuring emails:

Message

Action

Details (apply the 5W2H principle: What, Where, When, Why, Who, How, How much?)

Evidence (optional enclosures or attachments).

The MADE approach is direct—it begins with the core of the message, creating a context and rationale for action and problem solving.

(Compare the MADE model of email writing with the AIDA model of persuasive letter writing, p. 48.) Following this approach will help the writer avoid the common pitfalls of many emails, such as:

- rambling, not getting to the point
- inadequate exposition of background circumstances
- insufficient definition of problem
- unsatisfactory definition of actual and expected roles of receiver
- insubstantial provision of supporting and explanatory material.

Figure 6.5 (p. 116) shows an email constructed using the MADE approach.

Editing email

Email programs have only recently begun to carry such standard features of word processing packages as spelling and grammar checkers. These checkers are still quite primitive but they serve a purpose, helping to improve the quality of your communication. If your email program lacks these functions it may be useful to copy a draft of important emails into a word processor to check for grammatical and spelling errors. Alternatively, you may compose the email using a word processor and, once you are satisfied with the quality of the text, copy it into an email document.

You may also find it useful to print out a draft of your email and edit and proofread it as you would a conventional, paper-based document. You can get maximum control over your writing by getting some distance from it, and a good way to do this is by printing it out and physically marking it up with a pen (resetting your text in a different, perhaps more legible font can also help).

[Electronic Mail] advocates love to push the benefits of direct communication. Managers send and receive messages on a one-to-one basis. Now that secretaries don't fix their sloppy writing, the whole world wonders how they passed English 1A.

David J Buerger

Figure 6.5: an email created using the MADE approach

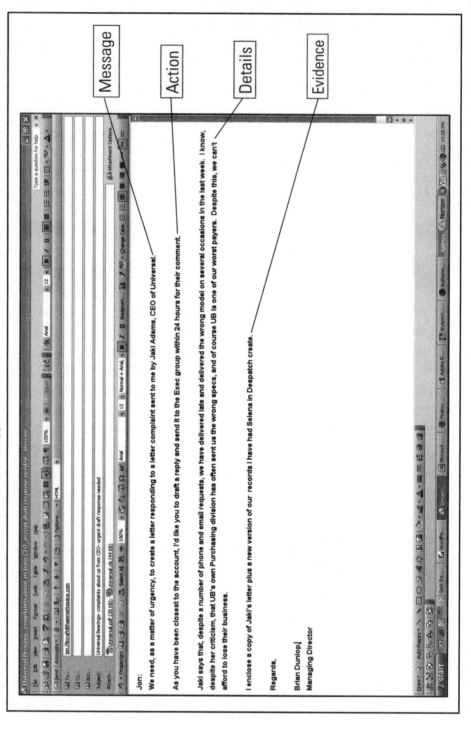

Jon:

We need, as a matter of urgency, to create a letter responding to a letter complaint sent to me by Jaki Adams, CEO of Universal.

As you have been closest to the account, I'd like you to draft a reply and send it to the Exec group within 24 hours for their comment.

Jaki says that, despite a number of phone and email requests, we have delivered late and delivered the wrong model on several occasions in the last week. I know, despite her criticism, that UB's own Purchasing division has often sent us the wrong specs, and of course UB is one of our worst payers. Despite this, we can't afford to lose their business.

I enclose a copy of Jaki's letter plus a new version of our records I have had Selena in Despatch create.

Regards,

Brian Dunlop
Managing Director

Message

Action

Details

Evidence

Layout and appearance

Following is an analysis of important elements involved in the layout and appearance of emails, including fonts, subject lines, paragraphing, attachments, links and identity details.

Fonts

In email it's wise to limit your use of fonts to one of the basic four: Courier, Times New Roman, Calibri or Arial. If you are using plain text formatting, you may be limited to the default font, without bold, italic or underline functions. If you use HTML or rich text formatting, you will be able to introduce variety and symbols, but bear in mind that, depending on their own software functionality, your readers may not be able to open up your email and see it exactly as you sent it.

Attention/subject lines

Try to include the most important information in the subject line. Remember, on any given day your readers may open their email inbox to a list of dozens, even hundreds, of incoming messages (many of them spam), and they have to make quick decisions about what to open first (and what to delete without opening). Your aim, then, is to motivate them to open yours first. Remember, with the limitations of most email package inbox displays, you will have only about five or six words of your subject line on display, so get the keywords in early (see table 6.2).

Table 6.2: choosing the best subject line

Uninformative	Informative
Meeting	Team 4—Special meeting, Thursday 6 June re poor results Prototype 5 test
Get together?	Thursday Social. Tut group—meeting/meal to plan assignment?
Client report	Universal Bearings—complaints from CEO—urgent draft response
Old faces	Pacific City High reunion—11 Feb 2008

It's also worth noting that, spam-hunting software may target emails with attention lines that refer to sexual matters, some financial matters and the use of exclamation marks.

Paragraphing, white space, numbering and bulleting

Computer screens don't give writers much vertical space in which to display a message before the reader has to start scrolling. The temptation, therefore, is to squeeze as much content into one screen as possible, which leads to a congested and cramped screen of text. Try to resist this temptation, and rely on the clarity of your message to encourage your reader to keep reading. Readers are more likely to scroll down a screen that is clearly laid out than to read and absorb information that is cramped and uninviting.

Accordingly, use paragraphing to separate key concepts, leaving a line space between them. In longer messages, consider using page numbering (perhaps using the format '2 of 6', '3 of 6') to help your reader. Bulleted lists can also help.

Attachments and links

Avoid trying your reader's patience with very long email messages. Attachments allow you to send more information by creatively exploiting the 3-D space in the email zone. Normally, attachments play much the same role as appendices in reports. Report appendices are usually positioned at the back of a document, they contain useful information, but are often too bulky and distracting to include in the body of the report.

At the current level of technology, it is unwise to attach files of more than 1 or 2 megabytes (MB), as many servers or computers that transmit electronic messages do not have the capacity to handle larger files. This limitation may be partly circumvented by:

- 'parking' supplementary files on a website, and creating a pathway to those files using an FTP hyperlink embedded in the email
- sending multiple messages with individual attachments
- saving the file material to a shared hard drive

- using compression technology, such as ZIP files, to reduce the file size

- using traditional delivery methods (post, courier) to send high-capacity storage units such as CD-ROMS or DVDs.

Figure 6.6 shows an email containing attachments and a hyperlink.

Figure 6.6: an email with attachments and a link

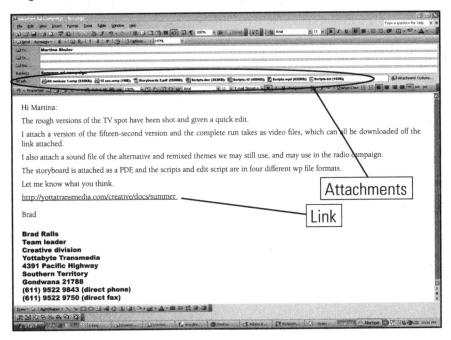

Identity details

Ensure that your readers know who you are. Remember, when your email arrives, the sender details may give your name, but not much else. You may decide to create an electronic business card and attach this to all your outgoing email. This is a type of attachment that can be transferred straight into your reader's contacts directory. These do not always work well, however; an alternative strategy is to create your own signature block, which you can insert into each email. When using a card or signature insert, include your:

- full name

- title or position

- organisation name

- other contact details (postal address, landline telephone number, fax number, mobile telephone number, company URL).

You may decide to use more than one signature block—say, one for official business to recipients outside the organisation, one for business communications within the organisation and one for personal messages. Example 6.1 provides some background to addresses in cyberspace.

Example 6.1: some background to addresses in cyberspace

Online addresses

Every website has an address, just like a street address. The web address is called a uniform resource locator, or URL. URLs are based on domains, which are sections of cyberspace devoted to specific types of activities and are identified by suffixes within a URL, preceded by a full stop.

Top-level domains include:

- .com—commercial or business organisations
- .biz—commercial or business organisations
- .net—organisations running a computer network
- .org—non-profit organisations
- .gov—government bodies
- .edu—educational institutions
- .mil—military organisations
- .name—personalised domain name
- .coop—cooperative business organisations
- .info—mainly commercial or business organisations
- .museum—museums.

These domain suffixes are often followed by a country code—for example, .uk (United Kingdom), .au (Australia), .cn (China).

A further domain level will often identify the organisation's region, province or state—for example, .vic.au (Victoria, Australia), .sh.cn (Shanghai, China).

Email addresses tend to be associated with websites (for example, customers wishing to learn more about <www.thebestsite.com> can email them at <info@thebestsite.com>).

When choosing a website URL and/or an email address, there is always a trade-off between the simple and concise or the definitive but long-winded. Long URLs and email addresses are specific, but they can be easily forgotten, or misspelt—and on the net, a single wrong letter, number or punctuation mark will mean a failure to connect. Educational and government bodies are often guilty of overlong URLs and email addresses.

The first country to go online was the US, so most US organisations do not require a country code. If you want your email and/or website to appear global rather than parochial, and to have the marketing advantage of being easily remembered, keep the address short. There are obvious advantages to having the email address

<kinross.bj@manitoba.gov> (24 characters) rather than <bertrandj.kinross@clientsupport.socialservices.metro.mb.gov.ca> (63 characters).

Email management

Manage your email by using the DRAFS (delete, reply, act, forward, save) system.

Delete as many unwanted or redundant messages as you can. Install spam filters to delete incoming junk mail before you even see it. Use your email package functions to set up rules to delete emails from people you don't want to hear from again. This usually means setting up a 'junk' folder and redirecting all unwanted emails into that folder, which you can clear with a simple block delete every week or month. Don't respond to junk emails by asking the senders to delete you from their mailing list. Response indicates to the unscrupulous that your address is 'live', and you risk receiving more, rather than fewer, messages from that sender and others to whom the sender has supplied your address.

Reply to emails as soon as you can, simply to clear the decks, but not too quickly and not too often. As email analyst Kristin Arnold suggests,

'Generally speaking, people who respond to every message within five or ten minutes are paying more attention to their email than to their jobs. When email has been lobbed back and forth (like a tennis ball) for more than three volleys, it's time to pick up the phone and go face to face'.

If a detailed response is required, and you do not have the time to do so within forty-eight hours, simply send a brief response saying you are working on it. When replying to an email, ensure that your reader understands clearly what it is about. Usually, there is a 'thread' or sequence of previous correspondence to place the email in context. Your email program may allow you to append your reply to your correspondent's message. If there is no such thread, set the context for your reader by recapitulating the circumstances of the correspondence. If the thread goes on at unnecessary length, delete or edit, or simply save the previous correspondence as a file and attach it.

Act on email using good time-management practices. Just as it is useful (if not always possible) to handle each piece of paper only once, it makes sense to use email as a tool for action rather than procrastination. Check out your email package's capacity to flag each item, so that your attention will automatically be drawn to it within a pre-set time.

Forward email to those who need to know about it. If the content is sensitive, check with the sender before conveying it to others.

Save important email just as you would save paper mail. Investigate the filing capacity of your email package. You will find that you can create folders and subfolders in which to organise your emails. You can also archive your communications either within the email package or to your computer hard drive. Establish similar electronic filing structures to those you use for your physical files and filing cabinets. Consider printing out hard copies of important emails.

Email—problems and opportunities

Email has had a number of positive effects on communication. Within organisations, it has helped to flatten hierarchical relations, breaking down barriers to communication based on position. People working at lower levels are more inclined to send an email than they would a memo or letter to someone of higher office. Email has increased the speed of communication, which is often no bad thing in bureaucracies drowning in paper. It allows the transfer of types of information (visual, audio) that cannot be transferred via paper-based correspondence. Email also allows *asynchronous* communication—that is, senders send messages when it suits them, while receivers open messages when it suits them. It can thus circumvent 'telephone ping-pong'.

Email also has several disadvantages, however. It has been said that the greatest cause of problems are solutions, and email may be a case in point. Some organisations have found that email traffic has exploded so dramatically that it has placed an intolerable burden on their networks, with the result that they have been forced to place restrictions on traffic to minimise email overload.

For some people email has rendered irrelevant more direct forms of communication such as using the telephone, walking down the corridor and talking, or attending group meetings. Also, many people are more likely to ignore an email than they would a letter or paper memo.

Email sometimes deceives people by its apparent informality, privacy, impermanence and speed—some email users will write things that they would never say in face-to-face conversation. But email is not private—legal decisions around the world have confirmed that the content of an email sent from the workplace belongs to the employer, not the sender. You should therefore be careful what you write—don't write anything in an email that you wouldn't write on a postcard, and don't write anything that you would not want to appear in a newspaper or be quoted in a court of law. Remember, even if you delete an email, the 'data shadow' of the email may be restorable on the network server.

Like the fax before it, email is sometimes *too* fast—it is easy to write things you may come to regret once you have given an issue more thought. Just as we can shoot our mouth off with intemperate words, we can shoot our fingers off with ill-considered writing. As the proverb states, 'Four things come not back: the spoken word, the spent arrow, the past, and the neglected opportunity' (Omar Idn Al-Halif).

Remember also that email is a relatively recent technology—ten years ago most people didn't have it (and if spam and other toxic internet phenomena get any worse, ten years from now most people may no longer be using it). This means that not everyone has email, so don't leave them out of the loop. Fax your message to them, send them a letter or telephone them.

Writing for the web

Writing for the web requires a number of specific skills. One useful skill, of course, is technical writing of code such as HTML (hypertext mark-up language) although WYSIWYG (what-you-see-is-what-you-get) website-building tools such as Macromedia's Dreamweaver or Microsoft's FrontPage now allow the construction of complex web pages without technical knowledge. Here, though, I am primarily focusing on online writing as a style best suited to communicating with audiences through web pages.

You as web writer

Web writing presents different challenges to other documents, such as letters and reports. In fact, web writing probably has more in common with scriptwriting for film, television or radio. Like scriptwriters, web writers are often part of a team putting together a complex artefact. The process can be involved and your sanity may depend on your understanding of the roles played by different individuals in it. As writer, for example, you may be involved in collecting client information from which to create the copy that will form the basis of the text. You will be involved in editing and proofreading tasks too.

Web writers tend to have more control over technical processes than film/TV/radio scriptwriters, who work only with text, with the creation of visual and sound images left to others. In contrast, web writers may need to be involved with the form and structure of the web page because of the objective needs of the text. For example, a web writer may need to establish the following sorts of guidelines:

- In this website, it makes sense for pages to be linked in this manner, because that is the way users will drill down from a particular link or image.

- In this online learning program, users will need to know about these three interlinked concepts if they are to acquire the desired competencies.

- In this game, players will need to know this information at this point, because otherwise they will not be able to proceed to the next level.

Figure 6.7 (overleaf) is a flow chart showing the role of writers in the development of a website.

Who are the readers, and why don't they read?

Any writing requires consideration of the audience. How do people read online documents? Do they read web text in the same way they read traditional print text? Website analyst Jakob Nielsen suggests that users of the web do not read at all—they merely skim and scan, picking out salient pieces, rarely reading extended text blocks. This may be partly because the experience of reading computer text is closer to that of watching television than reading print on a page. Online writing consultant Crawford Killian proposes that readers of websites are in a 'cognitively hyperactive state', a state in which they are simultaneously 'revved up', looking for 'jolts' or sensory rewards (click on this and see animation and hear music), and 'dumbed down', because the poor screen resolution slows reading speed by up to 25 per cent. (The visual resolution of a typical book is 1 440 000 dots per square inch, up to 277 times sharper than that of an average computer screen.)

Nielsen suggests that bad web writing and information design are characterised by:

- long blocks of narrative text, without paragraphing or headings, making it difficult to scan quickly

- overly wordy expositions of concepts, with more than one idea per paragraph

- obscure or 'clever' (rather than immediately understandable and informative) subheadings

- little or no hypertext or hot links

- hypertext that merely takes the reader to the text on the next page, rather than linking discrete blocks of related material

- indirect or delayed mode of exposition, with conclusions and payoffs offered only towards the end

Figure 6.7: website development—how the tasks of writers/editors fit into the process

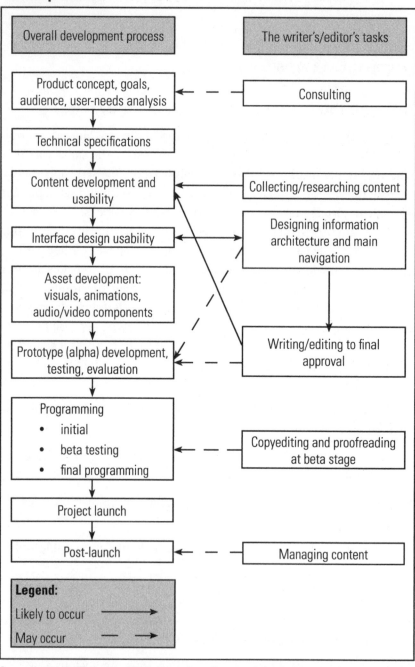

Source: Hammerich, I & Harrison, C 2002, *Developing online content: the principles of writing and editing for the web*, John Wiley & Sons, New York.

- 'marketese', or inflated and hyperbolic language
- technically complex elements (multiple animations, special effects, 'bells and whistles') that inflate file size and cause slow page loading
- inadequate/nonexistent site search function, which limits navigability
- inadequate/nonexistent site map, which limits navigability.

Using Nielsen's criteria, it follows that good web text will:

- be concise (up to 50 per cent shorter than comparable print text)
- be laid out in mosaic rather than linear style, with small blocks of text and headings
- be linked to other levels of related blocks of discrete text via hyperlinks
- feature one idea per paragraph
- be expressed according to the direct mode of exposition, with conclusions first (in the inverted pyramid style)
- use objective rather than hyperbolic language (that is, more hypertext than hype)
- highlight and differentiate points using bulleted lists, different fonts and colour
- be as technically simple as possible, facilitating rapid loading of page
- be supported by a good site search function
- be supported by a good site map.

Table 6.3 (overleaf) shows an example of how unsuccessful text can be rewritten according to these criteria.

Table 6.3: rewriting web text for maximum readability

Version	Sample paragraph	Usability improvement (relative to control condition)
Promotional writing (control condition)—using the 'marketese' found on many commercial websites	Nebraska is filled with internationally recognised attractions that draw large crowds of tourists every year without fail. In 1996, some of the most popular places were Fort Robinson State Park (355 000 visitors), Scotts Bluff National Monument (132 166), Arbor Lodge State Historical Park & Museum (100 000), Carhenge (86 598), Stuhr Museum of the Prairie Pioneer (60 002), and Buffalo Bill Ranch State Historical Park (28 446).	0 per cent (by definition)
Concise text—about half the word count of the control	In 1996, six of the best-attended attractions in Nebraska were Fort Robinson State Park, Scotts Bluff National Monument, Arbor Lodge State Historical Park & Museum, Carhenge, Stuhr Museum of the Prairie Pioneer, and Buffalo Bill Ranch State Historical Park.	58 per cent
Scannable layout—using the same text as the control condition in a layout that facilitates scanning	Nebraska is filled with internationally recognised attractions that draw large crowds of tourists every year without fail. In 1996, some of the most popular places were: • Fort Robinson State Park (355 000 visitors) • Scotts Bluff National Monument (132 166) • Arbor Lodge State Historical Park & Museum (100 000) • Carhenge (86 598) • Stuhr Museum of the Prairie Pioneer (60 002) • Buffalo Bill Ranch State Historical Park (28 446).	47 per cent

Version	Sample paragraph	Usability improvement (relative to control condition)
Objective language— using neutral rather than subjective, boastful or exaggerated language (otherwise the same as the control)	Nebraska has several tourist attractions. In 1996, some of the most-visited places were Fort Robinson State Park (355 000 visitors), Scotts Bluff National Monument (132 166), Arbor Lodge State Historical Park & Museum (100 000), Carhenge (86 598), Stuhr Museum of the Prairie Pioneer (60 002), and Buffalo Bill Ranch State Historical Park (28 446).	27 per cent
Combined version— combining the three improvements in writing style: concise, scannable and objective	In 1996, six of the most visited places in Nebraska were: • Fort Robinson State Park • Scotts Bluff National Monument • Arbor Lodge State Historical Park & Museum • Carhenge • Stuhr Museum of the Prairie Pioneer • Buffalo Bill Ranch State Historical Park.	124 per cent

Source: Nielsen, J 2000, <www.useit.com/alertbox/9710a.html>.

Try it yourself

1   Compare the online and print versions of a publication such as a newspaper. How is the same content handled in different ways in the different versions?

2   Use Nielsen's criteria to evaluate at least one website.

3   Visit these sites to pick up clues on how to write, and how not to write, online:
   • Jakob Nielsen's Usability Site

Try it yourself *(cont'd)*

- Vincent Flanders' Web Pages That Suck Site
  <www.webpagesthatsuck.com>
- UK Plain English Campaign — Website Design
  <www.plainenglish.co.uk/websiteguide.pdf>.

Conclusion

By now you should have a good grasp of how to put together an entire suite of documents, in both hard copy and electronic formats.

The more you practice the techniques and approaches looked at in *Business Writing*, the more adept you may — not will — become at writing in particular and communication in general. This may not only be good for your personal development, but also good for your professional advancement. The ability to write well is highly esteemed in workplaces, and the rarer that ability is in your current workplace or future workplaces, the more esteemed you will be — and that has to be good for you.

This claim may strike some ears and eyes as being rather far-fetched, so consider this. In 2000, the Australian federal government published a report, entitled 'Employer Satisfaction with Graduate Skills'. In this report, researchers investigated whether institutes of higher learning were actually teaching job-ready skills. The researchers concluded:

'If there is dissatisfaction with graduate skills as such, it probably lies in the area of written communication, because the majority of students are not taught to write in a manner appropriate to business communication'.

Irrespective of your educational background, if you are able to take the content of these pages and apply it to a range of documents, then chances are that others will notice — in the best possible way.

Good luck with the rest of your writing career, and don't forget to make your own luck.

Appendix

A sample analytical report

Here is an example of an analytical report. This one is just over 4000 words. You may be called on to write longer reports, but usually they will be shorter. Use this example as an approximate model to refer to when you need to undertake such a project, but beware—there are some faults built into it. These are listed after the report, but try to spot them before looking at the faults list.

Separate page for title.

Thought-provoking half-title. If the approach is more formal, then you would delete this.

Filling the void:
What is the best use for the vacant space on the ground floor of the Greenfields building?

Lay out page so that lines look balanced. Use illustrations if necessary. Consider placing within a robust cover.

Writer's name. Your name will be on your report, and copies of it may be around for quite some time. Make sure that it helps, rather than hinders, your career.

Target reader who commissioned the report.

Report prepared for Rocco Marcolino,
Chief Executive Officer, Agenda21

Prepared by Fran Powers,
Manager, Operations, Agenda21

6 November 2008

Memo of transmittal

> Or memorandum of transmittal. If the report is going to an external audience, consider making this a letter of transmittal.

TO: Rocco Marcolino, Chief Executive Officer

FROM: Fran Powers, Manager, Operations

DATE: 6 November 2008

SUBJECT: Options for allocation of space in Greenfields building

> Personal style, as befits a memo.

Attached please find the report you asked me to undertake on best uses of vacant space in the main building.

> Upshot of report is foreshadowed.

I look at a number of options, including the option that has been informally discussed for some time—namely, using the space to establish a fitness/wellness facility. On balance, I think this is the best option.

The costs are potentially high, but then so are the benefits. I have tried to recommend a pathway that will minimise risk and maximise positive outcomes.

> Courteous acknowledgement of others who helped out.

Max Franks in Operations and Jai Cellisi in Finance were very helpful in putting data together for this project, as was the information desk at West Pacific College library.

> Thanks to report commissioner, invitation to follow up with discussions.

This assignment was like no other I have tackled before, involving as it does so many intangibles, but it was a bracing and challenging one for the same reasons. Thanks for giving me the opportunity to come to grips with it.

If you want to discuss any of this material, please call me at any time.

Identify pages as you see fit. The scheme used here is to use lower case Roman numerals for all material prior to the introduction, from which point Arabic numerals are used. The cover is presumed to be p. i and the memo of transmittal is presumed to be p. ii, but are not identified as such. The table of contents page does not refer to itself.

iii

Table of contents

Indent different levels of report hierarchical structure appropriately — this allows the reader to see structure more clearly. As you prepare the report, this exercise may help you see for the first time whether the structure makes sense, or whether there may be changes needed. For example, is a sub-section really a new section by itself? Is the sequence logical or not?

Index needed? Possibly not for a document this short, but consider including one in longer documents.

LIST OF ILLUSTRATIONS

> Obviously not needed if you have no tables or figures. Better to have a good document without them than a bad document with them.

> It may make things clearer for your reader if figures and tables are listed separately.

SUMMARY

vi

Remember, that this may be the only section of your masterpiece that your audience will actually read. Forget about bruised egos and feelings of rejection — just make sure that you deliver a credible and persuasive message on this page.

Writer shifts from personal style of memo of transmittal to more formal and impersonal style. Match your style to the expectations of your reader(s) — for example, use personal pronouns if your reader(s) are comfortable with that.

This report examines various uses for the empty space on the ground floor of Agenda21's Greenfields building.

Four major options for use are considered:

- move out

- stay and sublease the area

- stay and use the area for warehousing

- stay and use the area for the establishment of a fitness/wellness facility for the use of Agenda21 staff.

Option four is the most complex, and thus most of this report is taken up with the analysis of the pros and cons of such a project.

Conclusions and recommendations are presented clearly. If you expect a hostile or critical response, it might pay to word this section less directly, trusting in the force of your argument to persuade your readers to accept conclusions and recommendations.

It is concluded that, while the first three options have some positive features, the best option is the fourth one.

It is recommended that a medium- to high-expense version of such a fitness/wellness facility be created. The venture should be reviewed after a three-year trial period.

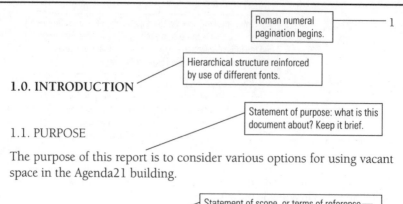

1.0. INTRODUCTION

1.1. PURPOSE

The purpose of this report is to consider various options for using vacant space in the Agenda21 building.

1.2. SCOPE

This report considers a number of options, including the option of converting the vacant space to a fitness/wellness facility. Only internal management of such a facility is considered; other options, such as outsourcing the management of the facility, or simply subsidising staff to attend commercial gymnasiums, are not considered.

1.3. SOURCES AND METHODS

Information was collected from books, professional journal articles, the business press, newspapers, websites, an in-house survey, and brochure and quotation material from commercial vendors of fitness equipment.

1.4. LIMITATIONS AND ASSUMPTIONS

There was some urgency in the preparation of this report, primarily because of the possibility of other tenants making firm offers on subleasing the space, but this has not compromised the analysis. All figures quoted from commercial vendors and other sources are assumed to be accurate, and survey responses of staff are taken to be a fair indicator of actual behaviour.

1.5. BACKGROUND

Statement of background. Useful for setting the scene. Can be a statement of the obvious, but sometimes that needs to be done.

2

The move to the Greenfields Industrial Estate building has been, on balance, a positive one for Agenda21. Our new building at 6–12 Main Street is attractive, and is easily the best facility we have worked in. We took on the lease at 6–12 knowing the building was too big for our current needs, but recognising the quality and ambience of the facility. The unexpected competitive pressure of bidding for the lease, combined with what appeared to be the certainty of a reliable and desirable sublease tenant, meant we signed off on the site before we normally would have. The sudden and unexpected financial collapse of our prospective tenant, Meridian, has occasioned a rethink about the best use for our facility, or indeed whether we should stay at this address.

Position all figures and tables close to the point in the text where they are referred to. Don't forget to refer to them in your text.

1.5.1. The current situation at Agenda21's Greenfields building

Figure 1 shows the layout of the typical floor of the building at 6–12 Main Street. The building is 48 × 32 metres/157 × 105 feet in size, giving a floor area of 1536 m²/16 534 ft², with all three floors (excluding basement parking and rooftop) adding up to approximately 4608 m²/49 600 ft².

Figure titles should succinctly explain just what the reader is looking at.

Figure 1: floor-plan layout for all three floors of 6–12 Main Street block

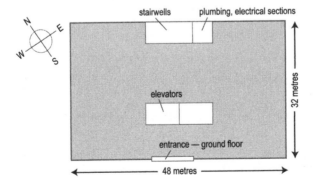

Currently we have 286 staff, with no plans for substantial growth above this level for the next few years. Our typical workspace requirements have

3

been for an average of 9 m²/97 ft² per person, with approximately another 1200 m²/12 917 ft² allowed for corridors/walkways, warehousing, cafeteria, library and utilities (elevators, stairwells, toilets, air conditioning, cabling, pipes etc.). Allowing for a small growth in staffing needs, this leaves us with approximately 700 m², or approximately half a floor, on the ground floor, unaccounted for (see table 1).

Table 1: space needs at 6–12 Main Street block

Area	Size
1 Total floor space	4608 m²/49 600 ft²
2 Space needs of approx. 300 staff @ 9 m² per person	2700 m²/29 063 ft²
3 Other space needs (corridors/walkways, warehousing, cafeteria, library and utilities (elevators, stairwells, toilets, air conditioning, cabling, pipes, etc.)	1200 m²/12 917 ft²
Spare space = 1 – (2+3)	700 m²/7621 ft² (approx.)

> There is no point 1.5.2. Some readers prefer that each section should have more than one sub-section, or 'twig on the branch'. Don't create a spurious sub-section just for the sake of symmetry, however.

1.6. APPROACH TAKEN IN THIS REPORT

This report considers four major options for Agenda21:

1   Move out to a smaller facility.

> Clear setting out of alternatives creates a context for decision making.

2   Stay, and sublease the vacant space.

3   Stay, and warehouse stocks in the vacant space.

4   Stay, and set up corporate fitness/wellness facility in the vacant space.

2.0. OPTION #1: MOVE OUT TO A SMALLER FACILITY

This is not really a viable option. We are legally bound to a seven-year lease, and the vendors, Imperia, are not sympathetic to our predicament. Legal action and penalties would cost us several hundred thousand dollars. Apart from these considerations, staff appear to have become strongly attached to the high-quality built environment, and a shift may have negative impacts on morale.

3.0. OPTION #2: STAY, AND SUBLEASE THE VACANT SPACE

We can sublease the vacant space to other tenants. Rates for rental/leasing of commercial property of this quality in this area are in the $180–$220/m^2/$17–$20/ft^2 range.[1] This means that we could recoup approximately $126 000–$154 000 per year.

Initial preparation would entail only partitioning costs of $2000 approx. The main advantage of this is that we would receive a substantial cash flow from tenants. Disadvantages may be that we lose control of some of our space, there may be security problems with non-company personnel in the building, and there may be territorial frictions (which commonly occur with leasing/landlord relationships).

4.0. OPTION #3: STAY, AND WAREHOUSE STOCKS IN THE VACANT SPACE

We are already warehousing some of our more valuable stock lines (Aegis 202, Aegis 303), but the rationale for this is tenuous. This building is really an office facility, and secure warehousing for even our premium lines can be obtained elsewhere. This would save us $17 000–$19 000 per year. The public relations benefits of being able to take clients through the warehouse section are considerable, but not decisive.

5.0. OPTION #4: STAY, AND SET UP CORPORATE FITNESS/ WELLNESS FACILITY IN THE VACANT SPACE

Many private and public sector organisations have in the past few years set up in-house fitness facilities, and perhaps the spare floor space could be used to accommodate such a facility.

> Definitions may also appear in the introduction section, or in a separate glossary, depending on what you are trying to get across to your reader.

5.1. FITNESS AND WELLNESS: DEFINITIONS

Some terminology definitions may be useful at this point.

> Proof that real facts are being cited here.

---

[1] Source: Max Franks, Operations Management, and newspaper and internet real estate sources.

5

'Fitness' is used here to describe exercise programs, which may entail weight training, aerobics, calisthenics/stretching, indoor sports such as table tennis, and cardiovascular routines such as cycling, stepping, walking and running. Many of these activities involve specialised equipment and (obviously) significant physical exertion.

'Wellness' is a broader concept, embracing all aspects of fitness set out above, but also encompassing programs such as:

- smoking cessation

- second-hand tobacco smoke control

> A list or sequence could also be treated in a sentence, with items separated by commas, or else in a table.

- stress management

- weight management

- nutrition programs

- alcohol and substance counselling

- ergonomic analysis of work practices

- occupational health and safety—injury prevention and rehabilitation

- corporate sporting teams

- time management

- assertiveness training

- interpersonal and communication skills training

- yoga

- massage

> Sources, with dates, help to establish credibility of assertions.

- meditation.

(Grant and Brisbin [1992]; O'Donnell [2001])

> Informal style of heading. A more formal version is: Effectiveness of Fitness/Wellness Programs.

5.2. FITNESS/WELLNESS PROGRAMS: DO THEY WORK?

The evidence on whether fitness/wellness programs work is mixed. Those who argue that the benefits of fitness/wellness programs outweigh the costs suggest that such programs lead to:

- declines in absenteeism

- declines in staff turnover

> Balanced approach, showing that all pros and cons will be considered, rather than a biased and unprofessional approach in which only one point of view is pushed.

6

- declines in injury rates (including work-related injuries and compensation claims)

- improvements in job performance and productivity

- improvements in morale and team spirit

- reductions in stress levels

- reductions in health care and insurance costs

- increases in recruitment of employees with a favourable attitude to both work and health

- cumulative benefits of US$500–US$700 per employee per year.

(Shephard [1999], Dinubile and Sherman [1999])

On the downside, the following negative aspects of fitness/wellness programs have also been noted:

- The capital, resource allocation and recurrent costs of programs can be very high.

- In many programs, only a minority of enthusiasts participate (and many of these were fit to begin with).

- In some programs, an initial wave of enthusiasm is followed by high drop-out rates.

- Health claim costs may increase rather than decrease if relatively unhealthy individuals self-select into the program.

- Costs may increase owing to exercise-related injuries.

- Productivity may decline, and discipline issues rise, if staff use fitness/wellness programs to avoid doing real work.

(Haynes, Dunnagan and Smith [2000]; Shephard [1999]; anecdotal evidence from discussion with colleagues in this workplace and others)

> More formal phrasing in heading. Less formal wording could be: Blood, Sweat and Tears: How Much Bang Would We Get for Our Buck in a Fitness/Wellness Program?

5.3. FITNESS/WELLNESS PROGRAMS: FINANCIAL CONSIDERATIONS

In looking at the costs and benefits of a fitness/wellness program, we need to consider the positive and negative cash flows associated directly with a program, and the flows associated with the broader picture.

5.3.1. Program costs and benefits

The setup costs of a fitness/wellness facility depend on what we are trying to achieve. Alternatives may include a rock-bottom, no-frills, unsupervised exercise area and a fully staffed and extensively equipped facility offering a range of services. Table 2 on p. 8 shows six scenarios that could be pursued (full details of these costings are given in Appendix A). A critical part of costing is staffing, and example 1 shows some factors affecting the staffing costs of a fitness/wellness facility.

Rather than clutter up body text with these details, the writer refers readers to an appendix section.

Example 1: some costs associated with fitness/wellness programs

- Casual trained staff (e.g. aerobics/yoga instructors, masseurs): ~$40/hour.

- Four hours of aerobics classes/day = $160/day × 5-day week = $800/week × 52 weeks = $41 600.

- Full-time (40-hour week, 40 weeks/year) fitness coordinator/director (with, e.g., bachelors degree in fitness/physical education): market rate seems to be ~$35 000–$40 000/year, plus on-costs (superannuation, insurance etc.) of 15% = $40 250–$46 000; median: $43 125.

Full-time (40-hour week, 40 weeks/year) medically qualified fitness coordinator/director (with, e.g., MD/MBBS degree): market rate seems to be ~$40 000–$50 000/year, plus on-costs (superannuation, insurance etc.) of 15% = $46 000–$57 500; median: $57 150.

Sources: *Daily Standard* and <www.workplacehealth.net>; internet job advertisements in health care/sports medicine.

Sources for data given.

5.3.2. Purchase versus lease/rent costs

Facilities costs here relate to outright purchase. These costs can be offset by depreciation (20 per cent per year), which can improve our overall tax situation. The lease/rent options can also be explored. Generally, leasing/rental works out at 23 per cent per year of outright purchase costs, and 40 per cent of these costs can be written off against tax.

Table 2: six scenarios for fitness/wellness programs

8

'Scenario' is used to distinguish choices from 'Options', but other terms such as 'Alternative' or 'Model' could also be used.

Scenario	Program	Staffing	Facilities	Setup costs ($) (approx.)	Recurrent costs ($) (approx.)
A	Simple exercise	None— unsupervised	Basic equipment (8 unmotorised workout stations, plus free weights in racks) No change rooms, showers, lockers	7 000	200
B	More complex exercise, including 4 hours/day group exercise	Casual staff (e.g. aerobics)— 20 hours/week	Basic equipment (8 unmotorised workout stations, plus free weights in racks) Change rooms, showers, lockers, reinforced flooring, glass partitioning, stereo	16 000	48 000
C	More complex exercise, including 4 hours/day group exercise	One full-time manager (non-medical) + 20 hours/ week casual	Basic equipment (8 unmotorised workout stations, plus free weights in racks) Change rooms, showers, lockers, reinforced flooring, glass partitioning, stereo	16 000	92 000
D	More complex exercise, including 4 hours/day group exercise	One full-time manager (medical) + 20 hours/week casual	Basic equipment (8 unmotorised workout stations, plus free weights in racks) Change rooms, showers, lockers, reinforced flooring, glass partitioning, stereo/PA	16 000	105 150

Tabular presentation good for complex and inter-related data sets.

Table 2 *(cont'd)*: six scenarios for fitness/wellness programs

Scenario	Program	Staffing	Facilities	Setup costs ($) (approx.)	Recurrent costs ($) (approx.)
E	More complex exercise, including 8 hours/day group exercise	One full-time manager (medical) + 40 hours/week casual	More advanced equipment—20 unmotorised workout stations, 12 motorised workout stations (treadmills, steppers etc.) plus free weights in racks Change rooms, showers, lockers, reinforced flooring, glass partitioning, stereo/PA	74 000	147 000
F	More complex exercise, including 8 hours/day group exercise, plus programs in nutrition, weight control, smoking reduction, stress management, massage, meditation	One full-time manager (medical) + one assistant manager (non-medical) + 80 hours/week casual/ contract	More advanced equipment—20 unmotorised workout stations, 12 motorised workout stations (treadmills, steppers etc.) plus free weights in racks Change rooms, showers, lockers, reinforced flooring, glass partitioning, stereo/PA, massage benches	86 000	216 000

Sources: brochures from three corporate fitness companies and three sporting equipment manufacturers. Full details of costings in Appendix A.

10

5.3.3. 'Low cost' options not necessarily cheap

Scenario A has the attractiveness of low cost, but the unsupervised nature of the program may mean that the company is neglecting its duty of care, which has negative ethical and legal implications. It is likely that such a program would also be 'preaching to the converted'; that is, it would appeal to those staff members who are already committed to fitness and not to those most in need of such a program. (There is also the possibility that such an unenriched setup may not appeal even to fitness enthusiasts, who may well prefer to exercise elsewhere, carrying the costs themselves).

> Thought-provoking phrasing: don't use if house style is very formal.

5.3.4. Skill levels of staff: a doctor in the house?

Supervision is probably essential, not only from ethical and legal standpoints, but from the point of view of giving confidence to those contemplating joining a program. Research on industry websites suggests that some workplace fitness/wellness facilities are hiring medical doctors, with or without sports medicine training. There is a salary premium involved here, but the presence of a qualified medical practitioner may add prestige and credibility to a program, and would obviously allow production of high-quality diagnostic information about health and wellness in general. Such a person could also contribute considerably to occupational health and safety programs already in place.

5.3.5. Possible impacts on key factors

It is difficult to come up with exact figures about what impacts, positive or negative, a fitness/wellness program may have on our workplace. Nevertheless, it is useful to work from the optimistic but prudent data offered in some of the literature (e.g. Grant and Brisbin [1992]; Kerr, Cox and Griffiths [1996]) and factor in some of our key figures, such as sick leave, absenteeism, workplace-related injury costs and productivity. Approximate estimates of potential improvements in these figures, as a direct result of the establishment of a fitness/wellness facility, are shown in table 3 on p. 11 These figures are based on median percentage changes possible; that is, the picture could be even brighter if, for example, productivity gains were greater than 5 per cent. Then again, the real situation may not be so rosy.

Table 3: possible impacts of fitness/wellness program on key figures

Category	Details	Approx. cost ($)	Median change possible, according to literature	Approx. benefit ($)
Sick leave (non-injury) taken in past 12 months	Average 6.3 days × 286 staff = 1802 days. Average cost (productivity loss, replacement staff) = $169/day	304 500	−5%	15 225
Absenteeism (when not sick leave-related)	Average 3.4 days × 286 staff = 972 days. Average cost (productivity loss, replacement staff) = $169/day	164 335	−4%	6 573
Workplace-related injury compensation costs (above insurance reimbursement)	Rehabilitation, legal	221 500	−5%	11 075
Productivity gain	Current output produced by total salary bill (average total salary plus costs = $50 000)	Salary bill = $14 300 000	+5%	715 000
Total				747 873

It needs to be stressed that these figures are hypothetical. In the real world, there may well be a negative outcome if a fitness/wellness facility were to be set up here at Agenda21. It may be of interest, however, to look at a very optimistic projection of outcomes to try to reconcile some of these figures. For example, figure 2 on p. 12 shows the costs of the most expensive scenario (Scenario F—equipment costs annualised at 23 per cent, with no adjustments for depreciation or tax benefits) against the figures from table 3 and the state and federal tax and insurance benefits discussed on the following page.

12

Figure 2: an optimistic projection of costs and benefits of a fitness/wellness facility

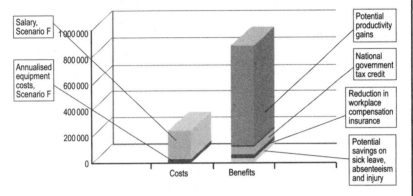

5.3.6. Non-program costs and benefits

Our general insurance covers any additional liabilities associated with exercise-related injuries.

There are several positive factors in relation to government-associated costs. Under new (2008) state government legislation, we are eligible for a 25 per cent reduction in our workplace compensation insurance, which amounts to 25% × $56000 per year = $14000 per year. Under proposed Commonwealth legislation, we can claim $300 tax credit per year for each person who participates fully in a workplace fitness/wellness program. If everyone were to participate, we could claim 286 × $300 = $85800.

5.4. FITNESS/WELLNESS PROGRAMS: NON-FINANCIAL CONSIDERATIONS

There are other considerations that may be important to take into account, although it is difficult to quantify them.

| Lead-in phrase doesn't say much, but provides a visual buffer between heading and subheading. |

5.4.1. Corporate Olympics

Each year we participate in the Corporate Olympics, although not with great success. A number of staff members have commented on the relative success of our competitors, Gigantic and Ramified Systems, in this contest, and in particular how Ramified's achievements last year led to substantial coverage of its team in the general, business and trade media. It is difficult to say whether such success really pays off in bottom-line terms, but it is not in contention that during negotiations with our reps a number of our customers raised Ramified's success. Both Ramified and Gigantic have in-house exercise facilities, which feature on their websites and in their recruitment literature.

5.4.2. Netball

We also sponsor the Hummingbirds netball team. The Hummingbirds have had some success, a number of the team having had interstate and international experience in the sport. Members believe, however, that it is difficult for them to maintain a high level of fitness as well as perform well here at the workplace, and have anecdotally expressed a strong preference for an in-house facility, which may lead to an improvement in their performance—decked out, of course, in Agenda21 Hummingbird uniforms.

5.4.3. Corporate sport and networking

A little-noticed part of our business strategy is informal networking through industry golf days and golf in general. Corporate golf is an important part of the culture of this industry, while other industries, for example IT, see sports such as hockey as non-trivial parts of team-building efforts (O'Keefe [2001]; Colvin [2001]). Anecdotal feedback suggests that our performance in these arenas of 'serious play' is not all it could be. It is not guaranteed, of course, but an in-house fitness/wellness facility may have a positive impact on the performance of staff members engaged in these 'off-duty/on-duty' activities.

5.4.4. Morale and teamwork

The workplace fitness/wellness literature also notes how programs lead to boosts in morale and teamwork. Also, some writers speculate that a reduction in staff turnover may be due to the perception of staff that a fitness/wellness facility, membership of which they do not pay for, is a perk, or benefit, that they may not get elsewhere (Grant and Brisbin [1992]; O'Donnell [2001]).

6.0. IN-HOUSE SURVEY OF POTENTIAL DEMAND FOR FITNESS/ WELLNESS PROGRAMS

If an in-house fitness/wellness facility was created, would anyone use it? The research data is sometimes pessimistic about short-, medium- and long-term attendance figures.

Reference to second appendix directs reader's attention to detailed data without breaking up flow of text at this point by including it all here.

A survey form was created and distributed via the corporate intranet (see Appendix B for the full text and results of the survey), using the question format 'If the following activity was available in-house throughout the day, how would you feel about it?' Some of the responses are shown in figure 3. On the one hand, merely because people say they want something or are going to do something is no real indication that they will actually do it; on the other hand, we received responses from 235 people (an 82 per cent response rate), which is the highest response we have ever had for a survey. (There is also the possibility that the true interest is even greater than the figures suggest, given that some staff may be embarrassed to respond positively to some activities, but would be interested in quietly taking up the option if the opportunity arose and others were going, or not going.)

On the basis of the responses, it is reasonable to conclude that a fitness/wellness facility would be well patronised.

Figure 3: some responses from the intranet survey, 16 October, 2008. (Number of responses = 235)

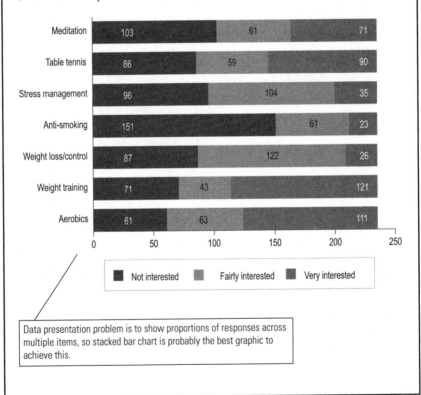

Data presentation problem is to show proportions of responses across multiple items, so stacked bar chart is probably the best graphic to achieve this.

15

7.0. THE WORST-CASE SITUATION: WHAT IF IT DOESN'T WORK?

Setting aside the possibility of catastrophic injuries being caused by participation in programs, the financial pain of a failed exercise would be considerable but not disastrous. If, for example, a three-year trial period was set, based on a moderate-to-high cost scenario, then approximately 60 per cent of equipment and hardware cost could be recouped by sales. Salaries, of course, would be non-recoverable.

> Some readers like an overview section, some don't. This could have appeared at the opening of section 5, but that may be premature in terms of the exposition of the argument.

8.0. OVERVIEW

Table 4 summarises the pros and cons of setting up an in-house fitness facility.

Table 4: pros and cons of setting up an in-house fitness/wellness facility

Pros	Cons
• May lead to substantial improvements in personnel health. • May lead to reductions in injury. • May lead to reductions in stress levels. • May lead to reductions in sick leave. • May lead to reductions in staff turnover. • May lead to improvements in morale, team building. • May lead to improvement of company image via more successful participation in external events (Corporate Olympics, sponsored netball team). • Will lead to reductions in WorkCover insurance premiums. • Will allow tax deductions under Federal Government Workplace Wellness plan. • May be attractive to future staff hires. • May help to limit company liability in event of future 'unhealthy work practices' claims.	• Only 'activists' may participate, or continue to participate. • Quite expensive to set up and maintain. • Improvements in health not always guaranteed. • Link between health and productivity not always strong. • May be expensive if less healthy staff participate and drive up costs. • May backfire if staff begin to sustain exercise-related injuries. • May reduce productivity and introduce discipline and coordination problems caused by staff exercising at inappropriate times.

16

> The conclusions section marks the end of the main part of the report and the beginning of the endmatter.
> Conclusions should be built on matter in discussion or body section. No new material, ideas, options or choices should be introduced here.

9.0. CONCLUSIONS

9.1. Options 1 (move out to a smaller facility), 2 (stay, and sublease the area), and 3 (stay, and warehouse stocks in the area) are not as attractive as option 4 (stay, and set up a corporate fitness/wellness facility in the area).

9.2. There is conflicting evidence about the financial viability of such facilities, but the balance of evidence seems to be in their favour.

9.3. There may also be a range of non-financial reasons to favour such a facility.

9.4. There seems to be considerable support among staff for such a facility.

9.5. In light of the range of uncertainties about such a venture, it may be wise to set up a pilot project, costed at a medium-to-high level, for a period of three years, and then evaluate it at the end of that period.

> Number conclusions either as subnumbers of section, or independent numbers (1, 2, 3...). Don't number at all if taste dictates.

> Recommendations are action steps based on conclusions.
> Recommendations should be built on matter in discussion or body section and conclusions. No new material, ideas, options or choices should be introduced here.

10.0. RECOMMENDATIONS

10.1. It is recommended that 400 m²/4306 ft² of the vacant space on the ground floor of 6–12 Main Street be set aside for the development of a fitness/wellness facility.

10.2. It is recommended that the Scenario 2 funding level be implemented. This entails the hiring of a full-time manager, with medical qualifications, and the hiring of casual/contract staff for forty hours per week. The facility will be equipped with twenty unmotorised workout stations, twelve motorised workout stations (treadmills, steppers etc. plus free weights in racks), change rooms, showers, lockers, reinforced flooring, glass partitioning and a stereo/ PA system. Salary costs will be $147 000 per annum (approx.), and a leasing agreement for equipment (rated at 23 per cent of $74 000 purchase price, or $17 020 per annum) will be negotiated by competitive bidding from equipment vendors.

17

10.3. It is recommended that the facility should run for a trial period of thirty-six months, and be re-evaluated against financial and non-financial criteria at that stage.

> Formal, impersonal style used. If house style allows, simply re-phrase to read 'I/We recommend that…'

> References listed alphabetically by first author. Author, date, title, publisher, place of publication given for books, author, date, article title, journal title, volume and issue details given for journals.

11.0 REFERENCES

Colvin, Geoffrey 2001, 'Why execs love golf', *Fortune*, April 19.

DiNubile, Nicholas A & Sherman, Carl 1999, 'Exercise and the bottom line', *The Physician and Sportsmedicine*, vol. 27, no. 2, February.

Grant, Carol Bayly & Brisbin, Robert E 1992, *Workplace wellness: the key to higher productivity and lower health costs*, John Wiley & Sons, New York.

Haynes, George, Dunnagan, Tim & Smith, Vince 1999, 'Do employees participating in voluntary health promotion programs incur lower health care costs?', *Health Promotion International*, vol. 14, no. 1.

Kerr, John H, Cox, Amanda & Griffiths, Tom (eds) 1996, *Workplace health: employee fitness and exercise*, Taylor & Francis, London.

O'Donnell, Michael P 2001, *Health promotion in the workplace*, Delmar Learning, Clifton Park, NY.

O'Keefe, Brian 2001, 'Corporate sports: is hockey the new golf?', *Fortune*, May 2.

Shephard, Roy J 1999, 'Do work-site exercise and health programs work?', *The Physician and Sportsmedicine*, vol. 27, no. 2, February.

Try it yourself: fault list

Here are some of the faults (deliberately placed) in the report you have just looked at:

- Not all sports/wellness activities are considered.
- The possibility of having an outside corporate fitness business run the facility has not been considered.
- The notion of simply paying for or subsidising staff to go to a commercial facility has not been considered.
- Can the company currently afford this facility?
- Despite the written disclaimers surrounding it, is figure 2 either 'too persuasive' (that is, might it deceive some decision-makers so that they commit over-hastily to a facility) or too implausible, leading some decision-makers to dismiss the whole concept prematurely?
- Do the figures make complete sense?
- What happens if staff simply abuse the privileges of the facility, and productivity declines?
- How will the facility fit into the organisational structure of the company?
- Is the structure of current headings and subheadings ideal?
- Have you discovered any other faults in the sample report?

Notes

P. 32: rules and applications—adapted from Lahiff, James & Penrose, John 1997, *Business Communication: Strategies and Skills*, 5th edn, Prentice Hall, Upper Saddle River, NJ.

P. 50: postscript—Ober, S 1992, *Contemporary business communication*, Houghton Mifflin, Boston.

P. 85: table adapted from Anderson, P 1995, *Technical writing: a writer-centered approach*, 3rd edn, Harcourt Brace, New York.

Pp. 105–106: Hobbes's Internet Timeline. Copyright © 1993–2006 Robert H Zakon <www.zakon.org/robert/internet/timeline/>.

P. 112: Baron, NS 2000, *Alphabet to email: how written English evolved and where it's heading*, Routledge, London/New York.

P. 114: MADE model—adapted from Booher, D 2001, *21st century tools for effective communication*, Pocket Books, New York.

P. 116: Screenshot reprinted with permission of Microsoft Corporation.

P. 119: Screenshot reprinted with permission of Microsoft Corporation.

Pp. 121–122: DRAFS model—adapted from Arnold, KJ & Biech E (eds.) 2000, 'Email Basics: Practical Tips to Improve Communication', *The 2002 Annual Handbook, vol. 1: training*, Jossey-Bass, San Francisco.

Pp. 122–123: quote from Arnold, KJ & Biech E (eds.) 2000 'Email Basics: Practical Tips to Improve Communication', *The 2002 Annual Handbook, vol. 1: training*, Jossey-Bass, San Francisco.

Pp. 125–126: © Irene Hammerich and Claire Harrison, John Wiley & Sons, Inc. This material is used by permission of John Wiley & Sons, Inc.

P. 125: 'Cognitively hyperactive state'—Killian, C 2000, *Writing for the web*, Self Counsel Press, Bellingham, WA.

Pp. 131–132: Department of Education, Training and Youth Affairs 2000, 'Employer Satisfaction with Graduate Skills', <www.dest.gov.au/archive/highered/eippubs/eip99-7/eip99_7pdf.pdf>, accessed 20 February, 2007.

Glossary

AIDA sequence: an approach to structuring persuasive documents (acronym for attention, interest, desire, action)

announcement memo: a message sent within an organisation to a wide readership or audience

appendix: supplementary material placed after the body of a report, where it is available for the reader to consult, without disturbing the flow of the argument in the main body section

attachment: a data file electronically attached to an email. It can contain text, graphics, video or audio in a compressed or uncompressed format

audience: the reader(s) of the report; the audience may be larger than you expect, including both official and unofficial components

bad news letter: a letter in which the writer conveys news that the reader will probably not be happy to read

bad news sandwich: embedding a bad news message within more positive information

balanced approach: an even-handed writing approach that avoids bias in what is presented or omitted

boosterism: a characteristic of reports that only focus on positive aspects of a situation, unrealistically ignoring negative aspects

broadband: high-capacity transmission channels that can carry multiple simultaneous transmissions

collection letter: a document sent to an organisation or individual seeking overdue payment for goods or services

complex sentence technique: a way of de-emphasising bad news by placing it in a subordinate clause of a complex sentence

conclusion: section of a report in which writers set out their opinions about the facts presented in the report body

decision avoidance: the behaviour of those who commission reports in order to avoid solving a problem

direct structure: used to deliver a 'good news' message in a straightforward manner at the beginning of the report

DRAFS: an email management system (acronym for delete, reply, act, forward, save)

drafting: writing multiple versions of a document, allowing time to reconsider, reconceptualise and re-edit each version until a final draft is achieved

essay: a document type that is concerned primarily with analysis rather than problem solving, and therefore rarely contains recommendations

extranet: a linked system of intranets that facilitates B2B (business-to-business) communication

flag-waving: a characteristic of reports that over-emphasise the value of the writers' departments, teams or sections

FTP: file transfer protocol, a process that allows uploading and downloading of files on a network

full block format: layout style in which all elements of a letter are justified to the left margin

good news letter: a letter in which the writer conveys news that the reader will probably be happy to read

hobby horses: pet projects or ideas given undue prominence in a report

indirect structure: used to defer the major impact of a 'bad news' message until later in the report

information/persuasion mix: the synthesis of fact and opinion in a report; information is concerned with fact; persuasion is concerned with opinion

instruction memo: a document, sent within an organisation, setting out information about procedures or operating routines

internet: a network of computer networks allowing the transfer of data and information between computer users

intranet: a private computer network operating within an organisation

job creationism: the process of a researcher/writer slanting the outcome of a report so that they will be the most likely candidate to implement the findings of the report

letter of transmittal: introductory or covering document for a report, used when the audience is outside the organisation

memo/memorandum: paper or email document sent to one or more recipients within an organisation

memo of transmittal: introductory or covering document for a report, used when the audience for your document is within the organisation

modem: a device (modulator-demodulator) that allows computers to talk to each other in the same way that a telephone allows humans to talk to each other

mosaic form: a non-linear approach to information design facilitated by hyperlinking — around and between web pages

persuasive letter: a document sent to an organisation or individual to influence or effect a change in behaviour

primary data: data created by the researcher

proposals, tenders, submissions: persuasive documents often used in situations of competitive bidding for scarce resources

reactivity: a characteristic of reports that only focus on the past

recommendations: final section of a report consisting of suggestions for action based on conclusions reached

report: a work-oriented document that is often used as the basis for decision making (and sometimes for decision avoiding)

request memo: a document, sent within an organisation, asking for solutions and action

scope: the terms of reference of a report; what the document is about, and what it is not about

secondary data: data already in existence, having been created by others

sloppiness: a characteristic of reports written in a superficial and unprofessional manner

summary: briefly sums up the content of the document; sometimes the only part of a report that is properly read

timidity: a characteristic of reports that do not tackle the real issues of a situation

topic loyalty: the process of a researcher/writer becoming so involved with an idea they are reporting on that they lose objectivity and will recommend implementation of the idea, when all the facts suggest that this would not be a good thing

vendetta: a characteristic of reports that unfairly ascribe blame to innocent parties

warning memo: a document, sent within an organisation, giving the reader a warning about his or her actions. Often only sent in hard or paper copy for confidentialty reasons

web page: a document on the World Wide Web consisting of an HTML file and associated graphics and script files; a website may comprise a number of web pages

whitewash: a characteristic of reports that avoid sheeting home blame where it is due

'you' attitude: approach to writing that prioritises the needs and interests of the reader

Index

If you found this book useful...

... then you might like to know about other similar books published by John Wiley & Sons. For more information visit our website <www.johnwiley.com.au/trade>, or if you would like to be sent more details about other books in related areas please photocopy and return the completed coupon below to:

P/T info
John Wiley & Sons Australia, Ltd
Level 3, 2 Railway Parade
Camberwell Vic 3124

If you prefer you can reply via email to:

<aus_pt_info@johnwiley.com.au>.

Please send me information about books on the following areas of interest:

- ☐ sharemarket (Australian)
- ☐ sharemarket (global)
- ☐ property/real estate
- ☐ taxation and superannuation
- ☐ general business

Name: _____

Address: _____

_____

_____

Email: _____

Please note that your details will not be added to any mailing list without your consent.